BUILDING PLACES INVESTORS BELIEVE IN

How to Attract, Win and Keep Businesses Investing in Your Region

AF884784

Paul Cranch

Copyright

BUILDING PLACES INVESTORS BELIEVE IN
Copyright © 2025 Paul Cranch
All rights reserved.

No part of this publication may be reproduced, distributed, or transmitted in any form or by any means, including photocopying, recording, or other electronic or mechanical methods without the prior written permission of the publisher, except in the case of brief quotations embodied in critical reviews and certain other non-commercial uses permitted by copyright law.

For permission requests, contact:
Local Economic Impact Advisory
Email: Paul.Cranch@ecdev.com.au
Website: www.ecdev.com.au

First Edition, 2025

ISBN: 978-0-646-73209-1

Design and layout: Paul Cranch

Printed in Australia

The information in this book is provided for general educational purposes only and is not intended as professional advice. Readers should seek professional guidance before making decisions based on the content. The author and publisher assume no responsibility for errors or omissions, or for any outcomes resulting from the use of this information.

Preface

Why This Book Exists

Economic development is often described as the art and science of creating opportunity but in reality, it's also the work of endurance.

It's about balancing vision with realism, ambition with patience, and data with empathy. It's about shaping the future of communities one decision, one partnership, and one investor at a time.

Over the years, I've had the privilege of working with councils, regional organisations, and state agencies across Australia, helping them design investment strategies, attract new industries, and support the businesses that already call their regions home. In every place, I've seen the same thing: extraordinary local potential and people working tirelessly to turn that potential into progress.

It's important to recognise, however, that many of the most critical investment decisions are made locally. Too often, the detail (and the art) of investment attraction is underestimated. As you'll discover in the chapters ahead, it's not something that can be done well by one person with a small budget. It requires focus, collaboration, and sustained resourcing to compete effectively. When done right, the returns from investment (whether greenfield or brownfield) can transform not just balance sheets, but entire communities.

I've also seen the other side: strategies and prospectuses that look compelling on paper but never quite come to life, projects that lose momentum because systems weren't ready, and practitioners who feel they're always starting from scratch.

This book was written for them.

It's for the economic development practitioners, council officers, regional leaders, and local champions who want to make investment attraction not just possible, but practical. It's for anyone who's ever been asked, "So what exactly is investment attraction?" and wanted a clearer way to explain it, demonstrate it, and deliver results.

Practical Guide, Not a Textbook

This is not a theoretical book about global economics or high-level policy. There are plenty of those already.

This is a **field guide**, written for people who actually do the work.

It's grounded in real-world experience:

- building investment pipelines with limited resources,
- managing community expectations,
- translating strategy into daily practice,
- and keeping projects moving when politics, planning, or fatigue threaten to slow them down.

You won't find academic models or abstract jargon here. You'll find plain-language insights that can be applied in any council office, regional development organisation, or economic team, whether you're managing billion-dollar projects or trying to land your first one.

A Book About Purpose

Investment attraction isn't just about chasing capital; it's about shaping the kind of growth your community wants.

That means knowing **why** you're attracting investment before deciding **what** or **how**. It means being selective, not desperate. It means building readiness, trust, and relationships that outlast election cycles.

It also means remembering that not all investment is good investment. The projects that truly endure are those that align with community values, strengthen local capability, and create opportunity without compromising identity.

A Changing Profession

The profession of economic development is evolving.

Technology, data, and AI are transforming how we find and assess opportunities.
Renewable energy and decarbonisation are reshaping where industries locate.
And the expectations of investors and communities are higher than ever.

That's why investment attraction today is as much about **credibility** and **culture** as it is about incentives or infrastructure.

This book aims to help practitioners adapt, to lead confidently in a time when the rules of investment are shifting, and to build systems that balance innovation with integrity.

A Personal Note

I've been fortunate to learn from hundreds of practitioners, in small rural towns, major cities, and everywhere in between. They've taught me that investment attraction is rarely about luck; it's about preparation, persistence, and people.

Each chapter in this book reflects that truth. It's written from the field, informed by the successes, setbacks, and small wins that make this profession both challenging and rewarding.

If this book helps even one practitioner feel more confident, one council become more investment-ready, or one region tell its story a little more clearly, then it will have done its job.

Because at its heart, investment attraction is about something deeper than deals.

It's about **building belief**; belief in place, belief in potential, and belief in what local people can achieve when given the chance.

Contents

Chapter 1

Why Attract Investment?

Finding Purpose Before Promotion

Every community wants investment, but not every community knows *why*.

It's one of the simplest and most important questions in this profession, yet it's often overlooked. Councils fund glossy brochures, governments launch trade missions, consultants prepare thick strategies, but very few pause to ask the most basic question: *What are we really trying to achieve for our region and our people?*

When you strip everything back, investment attraction is not about chasing logos or landing the next big announcement. It's about shaping a future that is more prosperous, more resilient, and more inclusive. The "investment" is merely the mechanism. **The true goal is community prosperity**.

When a region becomes clear about *why* it wants investment, every subsequent decision gets easier. Priorities become visible. Resources flow where they can make a difference. The team can even say *no* and know exactly why they are saying it.

The Bigger Picture

Investment attraction is often portrayed as a competition: a race between cities and regions for capital, jobs, and recognition. But it's not really a race. It's an act of stewardship, of managing your community's assets, land, people, and reputation so that they generate long-term value.

Every place has something distinctive. It might be a port, a university, a renewable-energy resource, or simply a sense of belonging that newcomers feel as soon as they arrive. Investment attraction is the craft of connecting those local strengths with broader opportunities. When done well, it brings in not only capital but also new ideas, partnerships, and talent.

The job is not to chase trophies but to cultivate a thriving ecosystem. Think of it less as hunting and more as gardening: creating the conditions for good things to take root and flourish.

When the "Why" Gets Lost

You can always tell when an organisation has lost its sense of purpose. The symptoms are familiar: glossy campaigns with no clear targets, frantic activity with little measurable outcome, and projects that sound impressive but add little long-term value.

One state authority I worked with celebrated the arrival of a large industrial plant that promised to be state of the art turning waste to energy and jobs for the local community. Within months the community was protesting. What began as an economic-development victory became a reputational crisis. The project itself wasn't inherently bad; it just didn't belong *there*. The attraction effort had ignored the question of fit.

When the *why* is missing, investment attraction becomes reactive. Teams respond to whatever opportunity crosses their desk, hoping that something (or anything) will stick. But credibility and trust are built on selectivity and self-knowledge, not desperation.

Knowing What You Don't Want

Clarity of purpose isn't only about the projects you *pursue*; it's also about the ones you deliberately choose *not* to.

Not every form of investment is good for every place. A town that promotes its clean air and lifestyle can quickly lose both if it welcomes a heavy-industry project that brings constant truck movements and machinery noise. A peri-urban community might see value in a large composting facility until the first summer wind carries odours through nearby suburbs. A small coastal town could accept a big-box distribution centre, only to realise later that it displaced the tourism and creative industries that made the town attractive in the first place.

Projects like these may deliver capital expenditure and a short burst of employment, but they can also erode public trust and damage a region's brand.

That's why defining *what you don't want* is as important as defining what you do. Early conversations with councillors, planners, and residents create a compass for decision-making. They help you articulate clear boundaries and communicate them confidently to investors. When investors know where they stand, they're more likely to respect the process and more likely to return with proposals that fit.

Some regions formalise these boundaries through land-use plans, zoning, or environmental overlays. Others set guiding principles, such as:

- investment must deliver a net public benefit, not just private gain;
- projects must support environmental and social sustainability;
- community liveability and regional identity are non-negotiable assets.

Having principles like these doesn't make a region "anti-investment." It makes it credible. Investors value certainty, even when that certainty means some doors are closed.

What Investment Really Means

The term *investment* gets used so often that its deeper meaning can be lost. In this context, it's not merely the flow of capital, it's a **commitment** between an investor and a community.

When a business chooses your region, it's not only signing a lease or building a facility. It's committing to employ local people, use local services, and become part of the community's story. In turn, your region is committing to support them, facilitate their success, and uphold the reputation that made them choose you in the first place.

This is why investment attraction is as much about relationships as economics. It's about mutual confidence and reliability. The regions that perform best are those that deliver on promises and stand beside investors through the life of their project, not just at the ribbon cutting.

Beyond the Numbers

Councils and agencies are under constant pressure to quantify results: how many jobs, how much capital, what's the growth in rate revenue. Those numbers matter, but they tell only part of the story.

The most transformative investments often produce outcomes that can't be captured in a spreadsheet: new skills, stronger local supply chains, more optimism in the main street. A modest renewable-energy project, for example, might create only a handful of jobs but position a region as a credible player in the energy transition, attract training programs, and build the confidence to pursue bigger projects later.

Investment attraction is about momentum, not just metrics. One well-aligned project can generate ripples that change a community's trajectory for years.

The Drivers Behind the Desire

Communities pursue investment for different reasons. For some, it's about diversifying an economy built around one or two major employers. For others, it's about reversing population decline or creating opportunities for young people to stay local. Some local governments simply need to broaden their rate base to fund infrastructure.

Understanding those drivers matters because it determines the kind of investment you should seek. A mining town seeking stability will target different sectors than a coastal shire building a creative economy. The clearer you are about *why* you're attracting investment, the better you can focus limited time, money, and political energy on what really matters.

The Importance of Alignment

When purpose is clear, alignment follows.

A shared *why* brings consistency across elected members, staff, and community. Councillors who understand the reasoning behind target industries can defend decisions confidently. Planners who grasp the economic rationale can work as partners instead of gatekeepers. Local chambers, RTOs, and universities can see where their expertise fits and contribute proactively.

Alignment also makes your strategy resilient to political change. A plan anchored in community outcomes, rather than personalities or electoral cycles, survives leadership turnover. It becomes a legacy rather than a campaign promise.

Attraction, Promotion, and Development

Investment promotion, attraction, and economic development are related but distinct.

- **Investment Promotion** builds awareness - it tells the story of your place to the world.
- **Investment Attraction** converts interest into commitment - it's the active process of engaging, qualifying, and facilitating investors.
- **Economic development** ensures those investments translate into lasting prosperity.

When these three functions operate in harmony, a region's efforts are amplified. When they're disconnected, each works harder for smaller returns.

Staying Focused Without Shutting the Door

Focus is essential in a world of limited resources. No team can chase every opportunity, nor should it try. But focus doesn't mean closing the door on anything outside your chosen sectors.

When an enquiry arrives from an investor outside your target areas, the professional approach is to treat them with respect and consistency. Take them through the same structured process (listening, qualifying, and advising) but calibrate the level of effort. Core-sector projects deserve deep engagement and dedicated staff; non-core projects may receive lighter-touch support such as data, introductions, or referrals.

Sometimes that means pointing the investor to a neighbouring region or another government department better suited to their needs. Sometimes it means keeping them in your CRM for future opportunities. Either way, they should leave the interaction with a positive impression. How you handle "off-strategy" enquiries says as much about your professionalism as how you handle your priority ones.

The Human Element

Behind every investment decision are people, executives weighing risks, families relocating, communities deciding whether a project fits their sense of place. Economic development is as much about empathy as analysis.

Investors will remember how you made them feel: whether you were responsive, genuine, and clear. Communities will remember whether they felt heard and respected. Balancing these relationships is what separates good investment attraction from great.

Measuring What Matters

Success isn't defined by the number of press releases but by the resilience that remains long after the cameras leave. The best investments build capability. They upskill the workforce, stimulate local suppliers, and give the next generation reasons to stay.

Real success is visible when your community starts attracting investment on its own, when the reputation for reliability and partnership becomes self-sustaining.

A Final Reflection

Before moving on to strategy or structure, pause to define your *why*. Ask yourself and your team:

- What kind of prosperity are we trying to create?
- What kinds of investment align with our community's identity?

- Which opportunities risk eroding that identity?

Investment attraction done well is not about chasing capital, it's about shaping a future your community actually wants to live in. The clearer you are about that now, the stronger and more consistent every decision will be that follows.

Chapter 2

Defining Success in Your Context

Turning Purpose into Progress

Once you've clarified *why* you're pursuing investment, the next question is *what does success look like?*

It sounds straightforward, but defining success is often where investment attraction strategies come unstuck. For some, success is measured purely in dollars, the value of capital expenditure attracted. For others, it's about jobs created. A few take a broader view, including skills development, population growth, or improved confidence in the local economy.

The truth is that *success is context-specific*. What represents a breakthrough for a small inland council may barely register in a metropolitan centre. A single new business that employs ten apprentices in a rural town could have more impact than a $200 million industrial expansion in a capital city. That's why it's dangerous to copy metrics from other regions without understanding your own context.

The Trap of Generic Targets

Many investment attraction plans start with the same template goals:

"Create 500 jobs over five years."
"Increase regional GRP by 10 per cent."
"Secure at least three major investments."

These numbers are neat, but they rarely capture what truly matters to a community. Worse, they can distort behaviour. If you're chasing job numbers, you may prioritise labour-intensive projects over higher-value ones. If you're chasing capital investment, you might welcome a project that uses a lot of concrete but delivers little long-term benefit.

A better approach is to start with outcomes rather than outputs. Ask: *What do we actually want our economy and community to look like five years from now?*

Success as Change, Not Just Growth

Growth and success are not synonyms. A region can grow (more people, more businesses, more traffic) and still feel worse off. True success is about *positive change* that improves the quality of life and opportunity.

For example:

- A council that reduces youth unemployment from 15 per cent to 8 per cent has succeeded, even if overall job numbers barely move.

- A region that helps local manufacturers transition to reduced energy costs has succeeded, even if the project count stays the same.
- A community that attracts a training provider to build skills in emerging sectors has succeeded, even if there's no headline major investor involved.

Measuring change means looking at *direction and durability*, not just size.

The Triple Lens of Success

To make success tangible, it helps to look through three lenses: **economic**, **social**, and **institutional**.

1. **Economic success** is the most visible — new jobs, private investment, exports, productivity. But these are the *outcomes*, not the purpose.
2. **Social success** focuses on skills, liveability, and wellbeing — ensuring that growth benefits the people who live there.
3. **Institutional success** is about the capability of your organisation and its partners — whether you're becoming more responsive, collaborative, and data-driven.

A balanced scorecard that captures all three gives you a much truer picture of progress. It also strengthens your political story: you can show not only that investment happened, but that it *made life better* and that your team is *getting better at delivering it*.

From Purpose to Indicators

Once you've defined what matters, you can translate it into indicators. The trick is to measure both the **visible** and the **invisible**.

Visible indicators include:

- number of investment projects facilitated;
- value of capital expenditure;
- number of jobs created or retained;
- increase in business registrations;
- rise in average weekly earnings.

Invisible indicators might include:

- investor satisfaction and repeat investment;
- the speed of approvals or turnaround times;
- the number of partnerships formed between local and state agencies;
- community sentiment toward investment attraction;
- stories of local people or businesses benefiting directly.

The invisible ones are often harder to collect but far more powerful in shaping behaviour. When officers know they'll be assessed not only on quantity but on *quality and trust*, their approach changes. They focus on service and relationships, not just the scoreboard.

Tailoring Measures to Place

Imagine three different communities:

A coastal tourism town.
Success might be measured in average length of stay, visitor spend per night, and growth in tourism-related training enrolments.

An inland agricultural council area.
Here, success could be supply-chain diversification, the number of new value-adding enterprises, or hectares converted to high-value crops.

A regional city with a university campus.
Success might focus on graduate retention rates, research partnerships, and the growth of knowledge-based industries.

Each needs different data, different targets, and different narratives. Using someone else's metrics is like borrowing their postcode, it doesn't fit your landscape.

Avoiding the Mirage of Big Numbers

Every economic developer feels the temptation to announce big numbers. It's what mayors want in media releases and what headlines reward. But numbers without context can be meaningless.

If a $400 million project lands in your area, the public will assume it's a windfall, yet much of that expenditure may leave the region through imported materials or specialised contractors. Conversely, a smaller local expansion may recycle 80 per cent of it spend locally.

Good reporting explains this nuance. When you communicate impact, don't just present totals; explain *how the benefits flow and who receives them*. Doing so builds credibility and protects you from accusations of spin.

Success as Community Confidence

One of the most underrated signs of success is **confidence**.

When locals believe in their region's future, investment follows naturally. Confidence shows up in small ways: full shopfronts, council planning staff willing to collaborate, school students talking about staying rather than leaving.

You can't easily measure confidence, but you can see it, and you can nurture it. Every positive story you share, every partnership you form, every business visit you make reinforces the narrative that "this is a place of opportunity." Over time, that story becomes self-fulfilling and a local narrative that builds local pride.

Measuring Along the Way

Success should be tracked continuously, not just evaluated at the end of a strategy period. Many agencies now use **investment dashboards** or **scorecards** updated quarterly. These tools don't just inform management; they create accountability and learning.

The best dashboards combine data with interpretation. For example:

- instead of just reporting "12 investment leads this quarter," include insights such as *which sectors are emerging* or *where bottlenecks occurred*.

- link every number to a learning question: *What does this tell us about our region's competitiveness?*

Regular reflection turns reporting into strategy development.

Maintaining Momentum

Investment attraction rarely moves in a straight line. There will be quiet periods, political distractions, or projects that fall through at the last minute. The key is to maintain momentum by recognising progress even when outcomes are still forming.

Celebrate small wins: a productive meeting, a site successfully prepared, a partnership agreement signed. Each one strengthens the system that delivers the next project.

Equally, recognise when something didn't work. Recording lessons learned, why a project didn't proceed, which competitor region won it and why, this turns disappointment into data. Over time, those insights become part of your competitive advantage.

Communicating Success

Defining and measuring success is pointless if you can't communicate it. Economic development teams often under-invest in storytelling, assuming that data will speak for itself. It rarely does.

A clear narrative helps your community understand the *why* behind your actions. For instance:

"This project didn't create hundreds of jobs, but it built the infrastructure that will attract them."
"This investment didn't come with a ribbon cutting, but it secured the university partnership that keeps our graduates here."

When people can see the logic and the link to local outcomes, they become allies instead of critics.

Political and Organisational Success

Economic developers operate in environments where political expectations shift quickly. Defining success early and gaining endorsement from leadership provides protection. It allows you to point back to agreed outcomes when priorities change mid-stream.

Internally, success also means building a capable, motivated team. Staff turnover is a hidden risk in this field. Agencies that invest in professional development, clear processes, and recognition create continuity and credibility. The maturity of your team is itself a success indicator; it's the foundation for every project that follows.

A Framework for Ongoing Evaluation

Think of evaluation as a living process with four stages:

1. **Define** — What outcomes do we want?
2. **Measure** — What indicators tell us if we're on track?
3. **Learn** — What do the results reveal about our competitiveness?
4. **Adapt** — What do we need to change next cycle?

Most strategies stop at stage 2. The best ones complete the loop, turning data into action. Over time, this creates a culture of evidence-based decision-making that investors notice and respect.

The Risk of Over-Promising

When the pressure to demonstrate success mounts, there's a temptation to claim credit for every positive development in the region. Resist it. Communities are quick to sense exaggeration, and once trust is lost, it's hard to win back.

Be proud of what you contribute but stay humble about what you control. Economic development is always a team sport, involving planners, businesses, state agencies, and some luck. Transparency about your role builds credibility.

Success Through Relationships

Ultimately, investment attraction is about relationships: with investors, with existing businesses, with the community, and with each other.

An investor who feels well-supported during setup is likely to expand later. A councillor who understands your processes becomes an advocate rather than a critic. A resident who sees local people employed by a new project becomes a champion rather than a sceptic. The more advocates you have the better. You can then start talking to them about what they might need to help advocate more.

If your relationships are stronger at the end of a project than at the start, you've succeeded regardless of how the spreadsheets look.

The Long View

Economic transformation takes time, sometimes decades. Projects you nurture today may not bear fruit until after you've moved on. That's why defining success must include a long view: institutional memory, continuity, and reputation.

The most successful regions are those that build a track record of reliability. Investors return because they trust the process; governments continue funding because they see consistent professionalism.

When you think about success, imagine what you want people to say about your region ten years from now. Do they describe it as easy to work with? Forward-thinking? Resilient? That perception, more than any single project, is the legacy of good investment attraction.

A Final Reflection

Success is not an event; it's a rhythm, a pattern of behaviour, decisions, and relationships that compound over time.

Chapter 3

Understanding the Types of Investment

The Building Blocks of a Strategic Pipeline

Once you've clarified *why* investment matters and *what success looks like* for your community, the next question becomes: **what kind of investment are you actually trying to attract?**

This might sound obvious, but it's one of the most overlooked questions in economic development. Too often, teams chase projects indiscriminately, treating every enquiry as a good one. In reality, each type of investment behaves differently, it follows its own timelines, carries its own risks, and contributes differently to the local economy.

Understanding these differences is what separates a reactive team from a strategic one. The most successful investment professionals can instantly identify what kind of project they're dealing with and tailor their facilitation accordingly. They know that not all dollars deliver equal value, and that the "best" project is the one that aligns with the region's assets, identity, and long-term vision.

The Many Faces of Investment

When we talk about "investment," it's easy to picture a single image, a new factory rising from a paddock, a logistics warehouse, a renewable energy site. But in practice, investment takes many forms, and each one demands a slightly different playbook.

Broadly, we can group investment opportunities into seven main categories:

1. **Greenfield investment** – building from the ground up on undeveloped land.
2. **Brownfield investment** – redeveloping or repurposing existing sites or facilities.
3. **Expansion investment** – growing or diversifying existing local businesses.
4. **Joint ventures and partnerships** – sharing risk and resources between local and external players.
5. **Mergers and acquisitions (M&A)** – investors purchasing or consolidating existing firms.
6. **Infrastructure and precinct investments** – large-scale enabling projects, often public–private.

7. **Domestic reinvestment and entrepreneurship** – the homegrown investment that sustains long-term prosperity.

These categories aren't rigid boxes, but they provide a useful framework for strategy, resourcing, and communication. Each tells a different story about how your region is evolving and each demands a slightly different kind of support.

1. Greenfield Investment – Building from the Ground Up

Greenfield projects are the most visible and often the most celebrated. They occur when a company decides to establish a completely new operation in your region, a manufacturing plant, data centre, research hub, or logistics facility.

For communities, these projects can be transformative. They bring new employment, supply-chain activity, infrastructure upgrades, and often a renewed sense of optimism. A single greenfield development can shift a region's trajectory for decades.

But with opportunity comes complexity. Greenfield investors are making high-risk decisions and will scrutinise every element, from workforce skills and utility capacity to zoning, planning approval timelines, and political stability. They expect clarity, speed, and certainty.

If your region isn't investment-ready, if zoning is uncertain, utilities are stretched, or council departments aren't aligned, the opportunity may quietly move elsewhere.

In practice, winning a greenfield project means doing the groundwork years in advance: preparing sites, establishing "one-stop-shop" processes, and maintaining relationships with agencies that control permitting or infrastructure.

When these pieces align, the payoff is enormous. When they don't, it can expose a region's weaknesses in full public view.

2. Brownfield Investment – Breathing New Life into Old Places

While greenfield projects tend to grab headlines, **brownfield investments** often deliver the most sustainable and community-friendly outcomes.

A brownfield investment involves reusing, upgrading, or repurposing an existing facility or industrial site. The land has typically been developed before sometimes recently, sometimes decades ago and may require remediation or reconfiguration.

For investors, brownfield sites can reduce cost and time. Roads, utilities, and access are usually already in place, and planning frameworks may be more flexible than in untouched areas. For councils, brownfield projects are an opportunity to revitalise underused land, reduce sprawl, and signal a commitment to sustainability by "building new on the old."

These projects, however, come with their own complexities. Old sites can carry environmental legacies such as soil contamination or asbestos. Heritage protections may limit redevelopment options. Communities may support renewal in principle but resist specific uses; for example, a former industrial estate being converted into a transport depot or recycling facility that raises concerns about truck movements or noise.

The role of the practitioner is to broker trust and clarity. You must help investors see the opportunity while helping communities see the benefit. The success of brownfield investment often depends on how well you communicate the transformation story: from dereliction to productivity, from risk to renewal.

Across Australia, we've seen brilliant examples, abandoned rail yards turned into logistics hubs, decommissioned fire stations repurposed into innovation hubs, and disused warehouses reborn as co-working and innovation spaces.

Brownfield investment sits at the intersection of *attraction* and *regeneration*. It preserves the bones of the past while preparing the ground for the industries of the future. In an era of limited land and rising environmental consciousness, this form of investment is becoming increasingly central to regional competitiveness.

3. Expansion Investment – The Often-Ignored Goldmine

While greenfield and brownfield projects create buzz, the reality is that most new jobs and capital come from **expansion by existing investors.**

These are the companies that already operate in your region, the ones who know the community, employ locals, and have already chosen your place once. When they expand, the benefits flow quickly: construction work, new suppliers, and local credibility.

Yet expansion investment is often underappreciated. Because it lacks novelty, it rarely makes the front page. But these projects are usually lower risk, easier to facilitate, and faster to deliver. They also send an important message to the market: that companies already here are confident enough to double down.

For investment practitioners, this is the goldmine hiding in plain sight. Regular contact with local businesses, through aftercare programs, business visits, or advisory networks is what keeps expansion opportunities visible. When a company feels supported, they're more likely to reinvest locally rather than relocate or expand elsewhere.

An effective attraction strategy doesn't separate "new" and "existing" investors; it integrates them. Today's new investor is tomorrow's existing one and how you treat them now determines whether they grow with you later.

4. Joint Ventures and Partnerships – Sharing the Load

Some of the most exciting and resilient projects come from **collaboration**. Joint ventures bring together local and external partners to share capital, expertise, and risk.

For example, a renewable-energy developer might partner with a local council to establish a solar precinct on underused land. A university could join forces with a multinational firm to create a research and training hub. A local agribusiness might team up with an overseas company to establish a cold storage export facility.

These partnerships create shared ownership and local participation, both critical for community buy-in and long-term success. But they require careful facilitation. Different partners bring different objectives, governance structures, and cultural expectations.

Practitioners play a vital bridging role: aligning interests, clarifying responsibilities, and ensuring that agreements reflect mutual benefit. Joint ventures thrive when everyone contributes something unique, capital from one side, local knowledge and networks from the other and when trust is built through transparency.

5. Mergers and Acquisitions – Quiet but Powerful Forms of Investment

Not all investment looks like construction. Some of the most significant economic shifts happen through **Mergers & Acquisitions** (M&A), when investors buy or merge with existing companies.

These transactions can inject new life into local businesses by providing capital, technology, and access to global markets. They can also, however, cause disruption like workforce restructuring, loss of local control, or community anxiety about foreign ownership.

Economic developers may not control these deals, but they can influence outcomes. Maintaining visibility over local industry movements, supporting transitions, and facilitating introductions can ensure acquisitions strengthen rather than hollow out the local economy.

Some forward-thinking agencies are even courting M&A intentionally like matching high-performing local firms with potential investors or partners abroad. Done transparently and strategically, this kind of matchmaking can generate growth without the disruption of relocation or new land use.

6. Infrastructure and Precinct Investments – Foundations for the Future

Infrastructure investments are the scaffolding of regional competitiveness. They include everything from airports and industrial estates to broadband networks and renewable-energy zones.

These projects are often joint ventures between public and private sectors and usually take years, sometimes decades, to plan and deliver. They're not glamorous, but they're the reason other investments can occur.

An industrial precinct, for instance, might not look like a single project, but over time it can host dozens of private businesses, creating exponential value. A logistics hub might start as a government initiative but quickly attract warehousing, transport, and technology companies.

Your role as a practitioner is to help turn infrastructure from a "government cost" into a "community investment." That means aligning partners, keeping communication open, and ensuring that the project's benefits are clearly articulated, not just in economic terms but in how it improves liveability, accessibility, and confidence.

7. Domestic Reinvestment and Entrepreneurship – The Overlooked Engine

While international projects capture headlines, **local entrepreneurs and existing firms** remain the backbone of most regional economies.

A small manufacturing business adding a new product line, a farmer launching a value-added brand, or a startup attracting angel investment, these are all investments too. They may not involve foreign capital or major land use, but collectively they drive innovation, diversification, and resilience.

Supporting domestic reinvestment is strategic. These businesses already understand local conditions, have a stake in community wellbeing, and are less likely to leave when markets shift. They also form the ecosystem that makes your region attractive to outsiders. The service providers, contractors, and innovators that enable larger projects to succeed.

Investing in your existing businesses is the most reliable form of attraction. When local companies are growing, others will notice. Prosperity is magnetic and they have the potential to bring in associated businesses.

Why Classification Matters

Recognising these investment types isn't academic, it's the foundation of strategic focus.

Each type requires different:

- **value propositions** – what they're seeking from your location;

- **lead generation methods** – how they're found and approached;
- **facilitation services** – the kind of support they expect; and
- **partnership networks** – who else must be involved to make them work.

Understanding this allows you to allocate effort wisely. Greenfield investors may need data-heavy proposals; brownfield developers need site intelligence and remediation pathways; local expansions need personal relationships and fast approvals.

Without this clarity, teams burn time on mismatched approaches producing glossy marketing investment prospectus for projects that require feasibility or holding workshops when what's needed is land rezoning.

Matching Investment to Place

Every region has a personality its geography, workforce, industries, and values. Investment attraction works best when those traits shape the kind of opportunities you pursue.

A region with abundant land and renewable energy may focus on hydrogen, battery storage, or agrifood processing. A university city might target health technology, research, or international education. A coastal region could prioritise creative industries and sustainable tourism.

Trying to attract everything to everyone spreads resources thin and confuses the message. The smartest regions know who they are and lean into it. They pursue the investments that fit their identity, infrastructure, and social licence.

The Time Dimension – Quick Wins and Legacy Projects

Different investment types deliver value on different timelines:

- **Greenfield and infrastructure projects** are long-term and transformative but slow to land.
- **Brownfield and expansion investments** tend to deliver medium-term outcomes and visible within a few years.
- **Domestic reinvestment** provides near-term wins and resilience, sustaining activity between larger cycles.

A balanced pipeline should include all three. Short-term wins build credibility; long-term projects build legacy.

The Role of Aftercare Across All Types

Regardless of category, every investment needs follow-up. The real test of success isn't landing the project, it's whether the investor expands, reinvests, and advocates for your region later.

Aftercare is not a separate function; it's part of the investment continuum. It keeps the dialogue open, resolves emerging issues, and strengthens your region's reputation for reliability.

A Portfolio Mindset

Think of your region's investments like a portfolio. Each type has a different risk and reward profile:

Type	Typical Benefits	Common Challenges	Time Horizon
Greenfield	High job creation, visibility, infrastructure upgrades	Long lead times, complex approvals	3–10 years
Brownfield	Land reuse, community renewal, sustainability	Site remediation, heritage and perception issues	2–5 years
Expansion	Fast delivery, relationship depth	Overlooked, limited publicity	1–3 years
Joint Venture	Shared risk, innovation, local participation	Governance complexity, cultural fit	2–5 years
M&A	Capital injection, global market access	Loss of local control, job rationalisation	Variable
Infrastructure	Enables multiple projects, legacy impact	Political risk, coordination challenges	5–20 years

Type	Typical Benefits	Common Challenges	Time Horizon
Domestic Reinvestment	Sustainable local growth, inclusive benefit	Fragmented data, under-recognition	1–5 years

The goal is balance, a mix of steady local expansions, transformative anchor projects, and catalytic infrastructure. That balance creates both stability and aspiration.

A Final Reflection

Understanding the types of investment isn't about jargon; it's about judgment. Each form represents a different pathway to prosperity, a different rhythm of risk and reward.

The practitioner's art lies in matching the right investor to the right opportunity at the right time. Greenfield for visibility. Brownfield for renewal. Expansion for reliability. Domestic reinvestment for depth. Infrastructure for foundation. Partnerships for innovation.

When those pieces fit together, your region stops "chasing" investment and starts *curating* it, building a coherent portfolio that reflects its values and ambitions.

That's the point where investment attraction becomes not just a profession, but a legacy.

Chapter 4

Focus and Selectivity

The Discipline of Saying "No"

Every successful investment attraction strategy eventually reaches a difficult but liberating truth: **focus is power.**

Focus doesn't mean doing less for the sake of it. It means doing what matters, deliberately, repeatedly, and well.

A useful way to think about focus comes from the idea that *FOCUS* means:

Follow **O**ne **C**ourse **U**ntil **S**uccessful

The regions, companies, and leaders who achieve long-term success share this trait: they pick a direction and stay with it long enough for the effort to compound. In economic development, this discipline is essential. Meaningful outcomes require sustained attention, not constant strategic drift.

Economic development teams are often under pressure to chase everything: agribusiness this week, renewable energy the next, tourism after that, and maybe a data centre if the opportunity arises. The impulse is understandable. No one wants to miss out. But the irony is that the more you try to be everything to everyone, the less visible and credible your region becomes.

Selectivity, the discipline of choosing is what separates strategic regions from reactive ones. It's also what gives investors' confidence that you know who you are and what you stand for.

Knowing Your Strategic Identity

Before you can focus, you must understand your identity. Every region has one, even if it hasn't been articulated yet.

Identity is more than branding. It's the story that connects your place's assets, people, industries, and ambitions. It's what explains why your region exists economically, not just geographically.

For some places, the identity is obvious: a mining hub, a logistics gateway, a tourism destination, an education hub. For others, it's more nuanced and perhaps a combination of heritage manufacturing, lifestyle industries, and a growing service economy.

Clarifying this identity is the first step toward smart selectivity. It gives you the confidence to say *yes* to opportunities that fit and *no* to those that don't and to justify both decisions clearly.

When a community understands its identity, it stops being defensive about saying no. "Not the right fit for us" sounds confident, not cautious.

Why Focus Matters

Investment attraction is a long game played with finite time, money, and political attention. Every hour you spend chasing a low-fit lead is an hour not spent deepening relationships in your target sectors.

Focus matters because:

- **Investors crave clarity.** They're looking for places that specialise, not generalise. A region known for food production, renewables, or defence manufacturing will stand out far more than one that claims to "do it all", as there are certainly a lot of those.
- **Internal teams need direction.** Staff can't be experts in everything. Defining target sectors allows them to build real expertise, collect relevant data, and form partnerships that deliver value.
- **Partnerships become easier.** When your focus is clear, state agencies, universities, and industry groups know where to plug in and you'll be top of mind.
- **Community confidence grows.** People feel reassured when they see consistent, values-aligned decisions rather than opportunistic ones.

Focus is also a form of risk management. It prevents a region from chasing politically tempting but strategically weak opportunities, the sort that create noise, conflict, or long-term regret.

Defining Target Sectors

Target sectors are not chosen by whim. They emerge from a blend of **evidence**, **identity**, and **aspiration**.

1. **Evidence** — What does the data tell you about your strengths? Which industries already have critical mass, workforce depth, supply chains, or locational advantages?
2. **Identity** — What industries fit the character and values of your community? Which ones enhance your brand rather than dilute it?
3. **Aspiration** — Where do you want to be in ten or twenty years? Which sectors align with global trends and your long-term infrastructure or skills investments?

The intersection of these three elements and where the evidence of capability meets the community's identity and the leadership's aspiration, is your sweet spot.

Once those target sectors are agreed, everything else flows: your marketing story, your prospect lists, your data collection, even your partnerships and event attendance. Focus doesn't narrow opportunity; it multiplies effectiveness.

Clarifying What You Don't Want

Just as important as defining what you *do* want is defining what you *don't.*

Every region has projects that, while technically viable, don't align with community values or long-term goals. These might include heavy industries in lifestyle regions, developments that threaten environmental assets, or projects that generate little local employment.

Being explicit about these boundaries early, through policy statements, zoning, or clear communication saves everyone time and frustration. It also helps genuine investors. When they know what's off the table, they can adjust proposals rather than waste effort on non-starters.

Some regions create a simple "fit test" or investment charter that lists guiding principles such as:

- Projects should deliver a net community benefit.
- Environmental and cultural values are non-negotiable.
- Developments must align with regional land-use and industry priorities.

This kind of transparency earns respect. The right investors will appreciate the clarity; the wrong ones will move on, which is exactly what you want.

The Focus Paradox – Staying Open While Staying True

The danger of focus is rigidity. A strategy that's too narrow can make you blind to new opportunities or emerging industries.

That's why focus should be **dynamic**, not dogmatic. You're not closing the door on innovation; you're simply deciding how to manage your resources intelligently.

When an unexpected opportunity arrives that sits outside your target sectors, the goal isn't to dismiss it outright. It's to channel it appropriately and proportionally.

Handling Off-Focus Enquiries

Every practitioner has experienced this: an enquiry arrives that doesn't fit your strategy but still deserves respect. Maybe it's a niche manufacturer when you're focused on agribusiness, or a speculative property play in a zone you're trying to protect for higher value uses.

How you respond matters because word travels fast in the investment community.

The principle is simple: **be helpful but disciplined.**

- **Acknowledge and assess.** Take the time to understand the proposal. A polite conversation can reveal whether it's truly off-focus or simply a misunderstood fit.
- **Provide a baseline level of service.** Share data, refer them to other agencies, or explain regulatory processes.
- **Manage internal effort.** Allocate your best people to core sectors; handle off-focus enquiries through lighter-touch support.
- **Keep relationships warm.** Even if the current proposal isn't right, the company might evolve. Many long-term partnerships begin with an enquiry that initially seemed irrelevant.

This approach maintains professionalism while protecting your limited resources. It ensures every investor leaves with a positive impression, even if the outcome is a polite "not this time."

Balancing Focus with Flexibility

The art of focus lies in balance.

Be **focused enough** that your region's story is consistent and your pipeline manageable.
Be **flexible enough** that you can adapt when markets shift or new industries emerge.

For instance, a council that focuses on logistics may find itself naturally evolving toward advanced manufacturing as technologies converge. A tourism region might develop a creative industries cluster because artists and entrepreneurs are drawn by the same lifestyle assets.

The key is to recognise when these shifts are organic extensions of your existing strengths, rather than distractions. Focus isn't about freezing your strategy in time; it's about evolving with intent.

Using Data to Stay Focused

Focus without evidence is guesswork. The best regions use data constantly to test whether their chosen sectors are still the right ones.

Tools like business migration data, industry employment trends, property take-up rates, and supply-chain mapping can all reveal whether your focus remains relevant.

If a target sector is stagnating while another is surging organically, it may be time to recalibrate. Conversely, if an industry remains strong but you're not seeing investment leads, it may signal a marketing or facilitation gap rather than a strategy flaw.

Data turns focus from an act of faith into a cycle of learning.

Managing Political and Community Expectations

Selectivity can be politically sensitive. Community members and elected officials often expect every enquiry to be pursued, particularly when job creation is mentioned.

That's why transparency and communication are essential. When you have a clear, evidence-based rationale for your focus areas, you can explain decisions confidently.

Regularly brief councillors on your strategy, sector logic, and pipeline. Provide dashboards that show not just what you're pursuing, but why. When everyone understands the "why," they're less likely to panic when you pass on an opportunity that doesn't fit.

Community engagement also matters. Share stories that connect your target sectors to local values. For instance, how renewable energy projects align with sustainability goals, or how agribusiness investments support local farmers. When people see themselves reflected in the strategy, they're more likely to support it.

Collaboration Through Focus

A focused strategy also makes collaboration easier. When your priorities are clear, other organisations know where to contribute.

Universities can tailor training and research. Chambers can help identify leads. State and federal agencies can direct programs more effectively.

A clear focus doesn't isolate you; it invites alignment. In fact, it's often the key to unlocking resources beyond your own.

Focus as Reputation

Ultimately, focus shapes how your region is perceived.

A place known for "saying yes to everything" is forgettable. A place known for doing a few things exceptionally well becomes trusted and distinctive.

Investors talk to one another. If they consistently hear that your region knows its strengths, makes decisions quickly, and sticks to its strategy, you'll be seen as a safe pair of hands. That reputation is one of the most valuable assets you can build.

A Final Reflection

Focus and selectivity are not about exclusion, they're about intention.

They're about understanding who you are as a region, what kind of prosperity you want to create, and how to protect the credibility that makes investment possible in the first place.

The discipline to focus is what transforms investment attraction from an act of chance into an act of leadership. It's what allows you to say to your community, "**We're not chasing everything, we're chasing the right things**."

And when you get that right, you stop reacting to opportunities and start shaping them.

Chapter 5

Measuring Impact and Maintaining Momentum

Turning Strategy into Evidence and Energy

One of the most common questions practitioners hear from elected officials or the public is,

"How do we know if all this investment attraction work is actually working?"

It's a fair question. Investment attraction is a long game. Deals take years to mature, and much of the groundwork (the networking, the data preparation, the quiet investor conversations) happens out of sight. Without a clear framework for measuring impact, even strong programs can look uncertain or underperforming to outsiders.

That's why measurement isn't just about accountability. It's about confidence, political, organisational, and community confidence that the effort is producing tangible outcomes and positioning the region for long-term prosperity.

Why Measurement Matters

Measurement gives shape to ambition. It turns purpose into something visible, repeatable, and defensible.

Without metrics, every discussion becomes subjective: "We feel like things are going well" or "It seems quiet this quarter." With metrics, you can show progress even in the quieter phases between announcements.

But good measurement goes beyond counting ribbon-cuttings. It tracks the *health* of the entire investment ecosystem, the pipelines, partnerships, processes, and perceptions that make investment possible.

Measurement also builds resilience. When a project falls through, you can demonstrate that the system still worked: the region was considered, the investor's experience was positive, lessons were captured, and the next opportunity will be easier to win.

From Activity to Impact

A common mistake is to confuse **activity** with **impact**. Activity is what you do: meetings, events, leads, reports. Impact is what changes as a result: jobs, business confidence, infrastructure use, skills, and reputation.

Activity metrics tell you whether you're busy. Impact metrics tell you whether you're effective.

Both matters, but they serve different purposes. Activity measures help manage workflow and demonstrate responsiveness. Impact measures help evaluate strategy and justify investment of public funds.

The art lies in linking the two. Every activity should trace to an outcome, and every outcome should link back to a purpose.

Building an Investment Performance Framework

A good performance framework answers four questions:

1. **What are we trying to achieve?**
   Define clear objectives derived from your "why." Examples: increase the diversity of local industries, attract new capital to priority sectors, or strengthen aftercare and reinvestment.

2. **How will we measure progress?**
   Identify both quantitative and qualitative indicators.

3. **How will we collect and report data?**
   Establish consistent systems so results can be verified and compared over time.

4. **How will we learn and adapt?**
   Treat measurement as a feedback loop, not a scoreboard.

When these questions are answered collectively by your team and leadership, measurement shifts from a compliance exercise to a management tool.

Designing Meaningful Indicators

1. Output Indicators – What You Do

These show operational delivery:

- number of investment leads generated or managed;
- response time to enquiries;
- site visits organised;
- events, briefings, or business engagements delivered;
- marketing campaigns executed.

They demonstrate capacity and efficiency and how well your team functions as a service provider.

2. Outcome Indicators – What Changes

These show tangible results:

- value of capital expenditure facilitated;
- jobs created or retained;
- number of local suppliers engaged;
- growth in target-sector employment;
- percentage of investors choosing to reinvest or expand.

These are the metrics leaders and media usually want, but they only make sense when interpreted in context.

3. Impact Indicators – Why It Matters

Impact indicators connect economic development to community wellbeing:

- increase in household income or business confidence;
- improvement in regional reputation or visibility;
- enhanced workforce skills and training participation;
- improved infrastructure utilisation;
- community sentiment toward local growth.

These measures take longer to show movement but tell the deeper story of transformation.

The Power of Leading and Lagging Indicators

Not every measure moves at the same speed. Some are **leading indicators** and early signs of future success. Others are **lagging indicators**, results that appear months or years later.

Leading indicators might include:

- number of qualified leads in your pipeline;
- percentage of enquiries converted to site visits;
- average investor satisfaction score;
- new partnerships or MOUs signed.

Lagging indicators include:

- total capital investment landed;
- new jobs created;
- export volumes;
- increase in local GDP.

Balancing both gives a full picture. When leading indicators trend positively, you can show progress even before major projects materialise which will keep stakeholders patient and motivated.

Turning Numbers into Narratives

Data alone rarely wins hearts or budgets. Numbers become powerful when paired with stories that illustrate their meaning.

Instead of simply reporting “three investment projects landed,” describe what they *represent*:

“Three projects across advanced manufacturing and agrifood created 86 local jobs and reactivated a previously vacant industrial estate. Each company has committed to using local suppliers and training apprentices.”

Stories connect data to people. They make measurement tangible and politically durable.

Collect quotes, photographs, and small wins throughout the year so you’re not scrambling for examples later. Build a habit of celebrating incremental progress, every site visit, every satisfied investor, every student hired because a new business opened its doors.

Dashboards and Reporting

The best councils and agencies use simple dashboards, visual tools that track key metrics quarterly. A good dashboard:

- includes no more than a dozen core measures;
- mixes quantitative data with short qualitative insights;
- links each metric to a strategic goal;
- shows trend lines, not just single data points;
- is shared internally and externally.

Dashboards keep momentum alive between big announcements. They also foster accountability: when the data is visible, performance improves naturally.

If resources allow, integrate your dashboard with your CRM or project-management system so staff can update metrics as they go rather than retrofitting data at year-end.

Measuring Collaboration and Confidence

Some of the most valuable results in economic development are intangible: stronger partnerships, improved cross-departmental cooperation, and increased investor confidence.

To measure these, use surveys, interviews, and feedback sessions. Ask partners:

- Did we communicate clearly and early?
- Were your needs met in a timely way?

- Would you recommend working with us again?

You can also track the growth of collaborative activities: joint funding applications, co-hosted events, shared data initiatives. These are signs of an ecosystem that's maturing.

Confidence, though hard to quantify, is a powerful indicator. When investors and businesses speak positively about your region without prompting, that's impact.

Using Measurement to Maintain Momentum

Momentum is the lifeblood of investment attraction. Without visible progress, enthusiasm fades. Measurement keeps energy alive in three ways:

1. **It provides milestones.**
   Every indicator hit, every site visit, every partnership formed is a chance to celebrate and re-energise the team.
2. **It reinforces learning.**
   Reviewing results regularly turns setbacks into insight. If site visits aren't converting, investigate why. If a sector is underperforming, adjust your value proposition.
3. **It sustains political support.**
   Councillors and stakeholders are more patient when they can see progress on paper. Even partial wins demonstrate return on investment.

Reporting Failures with Integrity

Not every project will land. Investors change plans, markets shift, governments change.

Transparent reporting of failures builds trust. Instead of hiding setbacks, frame them as learning:

"While the XYZ project did not proceed, our region was shortlisted to the final two locations. Feedback indicated that our workforce skills and planning responsiveness were competitive strengths. Lessons have been incorporated into future proposals."

This approach demonstrates professionalism and maturity. It shows that the system works even when outcomes don't.

Building a Culture of Evaluation

Measurement shouldn't live in spreadsheets managed by one analyst; it should live in the culture of the organisation.

That means:

- starting every new initiative by asking, *How will we know if this worked?*;
- holding regular review sessions where staff discuss results openly;
- linking performance metrics to professional development and recognition;
- sharing outcomes with partners and inviting their reflections.

When evaluation becomes habitual, improvement becomes automatic.

Benchmarking and Peer Learning

Another way to sustain momentum is by benchmarking, comparing your region's performance with others of similar size or structure.

Benchmarking shouldn't be about competition or embarrassment; it's about context. Knowing that your average project conversion rate matches or exceeds peer regions validates your approach and motivates your team. If others are doing better, it prompts useful questions about what can be learned. It also helps you understand what other regions unique value propositions are and how to position your region.

Participating in professional networks also provides valuable data and perspective.

The Politics of Patience

Investment attraction requires patience, but politics rarely allows it. Elected leaders often operate on three or four year cycles, while major projects can take five to ten years.

Measurement helps bridge this gap by providing *interim victories*. Showing progress through leading indicators and stories keeps political leaders engaged long enough for the bigger outcomes to emerge.

Communicate frequently, honestly, and visually. Use graphs, maps, and testimonials and anything that brings the journey to life.

From Reporting to Advocacy

Strong measurement turns practitioners into advocates. When you can clearly show how your work contributes to the broader policy agenda (job creation, sustainability, housing, regional growth) you shift from being a cost centre to being a strategic enabler.

It's also your defence during budget season. In difficult fiscal times, departments with clear evidence of value are the ones that survive.

Measurement isn't just about proving success; it's about protecting capacity.

A Living Framework

The most effective performance frameworks are living documents. They evolve as circumstances change, new sectors emerge, old ones decline, political priorities shift.

Review your indicators annually. Drop measures that no longer add insight and add new ones that reflect emerging realities like digital transformation or low-emissions targets.

This keeps your program relevant and your story fresh.

A Final Reflection

Measurement is both a mirror and motivator. It reflects what's been achieved and fuels what comes next.

If Chapter 4 was about focus and deciding what matters most well this chapter is about proving it. Clear metrics, consistent reporting, and honest storytelling turn strategy into evidence and evidence into energy.

When your organisation can quantify its value, learn from its data, and communicate its impact with conviction, it becomes unstoppable.

Because in the end, investment attraction isn't just about winning projects, it's about building *confidence*: in your team, your community, and your place in the world.

Chapter 6

Setting Up an Investment Promotion Office

Building the Engine Room of Investment Attraction

Every strategy eventually needs a structure to bring it to life. The best intentions for focus, metrics, and community alignment will remain ideas unless there's an organisation capable of executing them consistently.

That's the purpose of an Investment Promotion Office (IPO).

Whether it's a standalone agency, a small unit within a council, or a cross-regional partnership, the IPO is the **engine room** of investment attraction. It connects vision with delivery. It's where relationships are managed, opportunities are tracked, and investor confidence is earned through responsiveness and professionalism.

An effective IPO doesn't just process enquiries, it **shapes perceptions**. Every phone call, email, and site visit is a chance to prove that your region is organised, capable, and easy to work with.

The Evolving Role of Investment Promotion

Investment promotion has evolved dramatically over the past two decades. Once seen as a marketing or public relations exercise, it's now recognised as a **strategic economic function** that requires data, diplomacy, and deep collaboration.

Modern investment promotion professionals operate more like **project managers and brokers** than marketers. They coordinate across planning, infrastructure, education, and industry to make projects happen. They understand their local ecosystem as well as any business consultant.

And because investors now expect speed, accuracy, and transparency, the IPO has become the region's **front door**, the single point of contact that turns complexity into clarity.

When the front door works smoothly, investors stay. When it's jammed or confusing, they go elsewhere.

One Size Does Not Fit All

There's no universal template for how an Investment Promotion Office should look. The structure should fit your scale, mandate, and maturity.

Broadly, IPOs fall into three models:

1. **Dedicated Agency Model** – A standalone organisation, often co-funded by multiple levels of government or industry. It operates with flexibility and a clear commercial focus.
2. **Embedded Council Unit** – A team housed within local government. It may combine investment attraction with business support, tourism, or economic development.
3. **Collaborative or Regional Partnership** – Several councils or organisations share staff, data, and marketing to promote a broader region collectively.

Each model has strengths and trade-offs.

- **Agencies** tend to move faster and attract higher-level projects but can be perceived as detached from community priorities.
- **Council units** are closer to planning legislation levers and community sentiment but can be constrained by bureaucracy.
- **Regional partnerships** maximise visibility but require strong governance to avoid duplication and turf wars.

The best choice is the one that reflects your resources and relationships and that you can sustain beyond political cycles.

Core Functions of an Effective IPO

Regardless of structure, every Investment Promotion Office must perform five core functions:

1. **Intelligence and Research**
   - Maintain data on sectors, workforce, sites, and infrastructure.
   - Analyse trends and identify emerging opportunities.
   - Translate raw data into investor-friendly insights.
2. **Marketing and Positioning**
   - Develop the regional narrative and unique value proposition.
   - Manage digital presence, social media, and investor materials.
   - Build reputation through case studies and success stories.
3. **Lead Generation and Pipeline Management**
   - Proactively identify and target investors in key sectors.
   - Manage enquiries through a CRM system.
   - Track progress from initial contact to project delivery.
4. **Facilitation and Aftercare**
   - Coordinate across government and utilities to remove barriers.

- Organise site visits and deliver investor services.
- Maintain relationships post-establishment to encourage reinvestment.

5. **Measurement and Reporting**
    - Collect metrics on leads, conversions, and impacts.
    - Report transparently to stakeholders.
    - Use insights to refine strategy.

These are the “five pillars” of modern investment promotion. Weakness in any one of them compromises the rest.

The Leadership Role – The “Connector-in-Chief”

Every successful IPO needs a **connector-in-chief** a leader who can translate between the public and private sectors.

The best investment leaders combine the communication skills of a diplomat with the operational mindset of a project manager. They’re comfortable talking to business executives one moment and community groups the next. They’re persistent but patient, commercial but ethical.

Leadership in this field is less about hierarchy and more about credibility. Remember Investors respond to people who are authentic, informed, and empowered to solve problems.

Team Structure and Skills

A strong IPO balances four key skill sets:

1. **Strategic Thinking** – Understanding sectors, competitiveness, and policy.
2. **Relationship Management** – Building trust with investors, partners, and stakeholders.
3. **Project Delivery** – Managing timelines, approvals, and reporting.
4. **Marketing and Communication** – Telling the region's story effectively.

In larger teams, these might be separate roles:

- **Director/Manager** – Sets vision and manages stakeholder relationships.
- **Sector Leads or Business Development Officers** – Focus on priority industries or geographic markets.
- **Facilitation Officers** – Handle logistics, approvals, and project tracking.
- **Research and Data Analysts** – Maintain intelligence and dashboards.
- **Marketing/Communications Officer** – Manages content, digital channels, and branding.

In smaller councils, these responsibilities might sit with one or two people wearing multiple hats. That's fine, what matters is coverage, not titles.

Scaling for Smaller Councils

Many regional or rural councils don't have the budget for a full investment office, but they can still build capacity.

Here's how:

- **Start with a clear process.** Even one staff member can operate effectively with a documented workflow for handling enquiries, logging leads, and reporting outcomes.
- **Leverage partnerships.** Work closely with regional development organisations, chambers, state agencies, or industry associations. Share data and coordinate marketing rather than duplicating it.
- **Use technology.** A simple CRM, cloud storage, and shared dashboards can multiply capacity.
- **Focus on aftercare.** Existing investors are your best promoters. Visiting five local businesses a month can yield more results than attending a trade show.
- **Outsource where needed.** Graphic design, data analysis, or international lead generation can be contracted in as required.

Investment attraction doesn't require a big team, it requires a clear process, consistent communication, and a commitment to follow through.

Governance and Autonomy

Governance determines credibility.

An IPO must be transparent enough to maintain public trust but flexible enough to respond at the speed of business. Too much bureaucracy kills agility; too little oversight risks waste or bias.

Consider three layers of governance:

1. **Strategic Oversight** – A board or steering committee that sets priorities and ensures alignment with community goals.
2. **Operational Autonomy** – Empowered staff who can make day-to-day decisions and respond quickly to investor needs.
3. **Accountability and Reporting** – Regular, evidence-based updates to council or funding partners showing progress against agreed metrics.

If your structure lacks one of these layers, decision-making will suffer. Either you'll move too slowly, or you'll lose stakeholder confidence.

Building a "One Door" Experience

Investors hate fragmentation. They don't want to chase multiple departments to get simple answers.

An effective IPO acts as the "one door" into your region, coordinating internally so the investor experiences a seamless journey.

That means:

- centralised enquiry handling;
- consistent messaging across departments;
- clear internal escalation pathways;

- unified data and contact management.

Behind the scenes, it might involve multiple teams (planning, infrastructure, environment, finance) but to the investor, it should feel like one cohesive organisation.

A “one door” system builds confidence faster than any brochure ever could.

Culture and Responsiveness

No amount of structure can substitute for culture. The culture of your IPO, how staff think and behave, defines its reputation.

Great investment teams share a few cultural traits:

- **Responsiveness:** Quick acknowledgement, even if the full answer takes time.
- **Transparency:** Honest communication about what can and can’t be done.
- **Collaboration:** No silos, everyone contributes to making the region look good.
- **Proactivity:** Anticipating investor needs rather than waiting to be asked.
- **Professionalism:** Delivering what’s promised, every time.

Culture doesn’t happen by accident. It’s shaped through hiring, leadership example, and reinforcement.

Technology and Tools

An efficient IPO runs on good information systems. Essential tools include:

- **CRM (Customer Relationship Management) System:** Tracks leads, interactions, and project stages.
- **Data Dashboards:** Visualise investment performance metrics.
- **Digital Asset Library:** Central repository for photos, maps, brochures, and case studies.
- **Investor Portal or Website:** Provides accessible, up-to-date information on sites, workforce, and lifestyle.
- **Collaboration Platforms:** Cloud-based tools for sharing files, notes, and schedules across departments.

Technology doesn't replace people it should amplify them. It ensures continuity when staff change and enables accountability when projects evolve over years.

Working Across Departments

Investment attraction cannot sit in isolation. The IPO must be woven into the wider machinery of government.

That means maintaining active relationships with:

- **Planning and Development** – to streamline approvals and anticipate zoning needs;

- **Infrastructure and Assets** – to coordinate site servicing and upgrades;
- **Education and Training** – to align workforce skills with emerging industries;
- **Environment and Sustainability** – to ensure projects align with regulatory and community standards;
- **Tourism, Business, and Events Teams** – to share intelligence and promote the region consistently.

An IPO that builds these bridges becomes an internal influencer, turning council departments into partners in economic development rather than gatekeepers.

Resourcing and Funding Models

Funding is always a challenge, especially in regional settings. Consider a blended approach:

- **Core Funding:** From council or local government for staff and operations.
- **Project Funding:** From state or federal grants for specific initiatives.
- **Private Sector Contributions:** Through sponsorships, memberships, or co-funded events or marketing campaigns.
- **In-Kind Support:** Office space, secondments, or shared technology.

Diversified funding reduces risk and fosters ownership among multiple partners. It also helps insulate the IPO from political turnover.

Training and Professional Development

Investment attraction is a profession and like any profession, it demands continuous learning.

Encourage staff to engage with leading peak bodies and consultancies that specialise in investment attraction. Host internal learning sessions. Share case studies.

Professional development isn't a luxury, it's insurance. The more skilled your team, the more resilient your program.

Building Reputation Through Reliability

Reputation is the IPO's true currency. Investors and partners may forget your brochures, but they won't forget how reliable you were when it counted.

Every deadline met, every follow-up delivered, every honest conversation strengthens your standing. Over time, reputation compounds. A strong reputation attracts investors who value professionalism and deters those who don't.

Your goal is for people to say:

"They might not be the biggest region, but they're the most reliable."

That's how you become a preferred partner rather than just another option.

A Final Reflection

Setting up an Investment Promotion Office is not about creating bureaucracy it's about creating *capacity*.

It's the structure that gives your community a voice in the global marketplace, the mechanism that turns strategy into action, and the team that keeps promises on behalf of your region.

Whether your IPO is a dedicated agency or a single determined officer with a laptop, the principles are the same: clarity, responsiveness, collaboration, and credibility.

Because in the end, the question isn't how big your office is, it's how effectively it can help others believe in your place as much as you do.

Chapter 7

Building the Investment-Ready Foundation

Preparing Your Place Before the Investors Arrive

At some point in every council or regional organisation, someone will ask:

“If an investor called tomorrow and wanted to move fast, are we actually ready?”

For many, the honest answer is no.

Investment readiness is often the missing ingredient between opportunity and delivery. You can have a strong strategy, a professional investment team, and a clear focus. However, if the foundations aren't in place, projects stall, confidence erodes, and credibility fades.

Being investment-ready doesn't mean having every site serviced and every plan finalised. It means understanding your assets, processes, and decision-making pathways well enough to respond quickly, accurately, and confidently when opportunity knocks.

What Investment Readiness Really Means

Investment readiness is the combination of **physical preparedness**, **institutional clarity**, and **community confidence**.

- **Physical readiness** means your infrastructure, land, and data can support new projects.
- **Institutional readiness** means your systems and decision processes are streamlined and predictable.
- **Community readiness** means your residents and stakeholders understand, support, and participate in the growth story.

Without all three, attraction turns into frustration for both investors and your own staff.

The Cost of Unreadiness

Every practitioner has a story about the "one that got away." An investor who visited, loved the region, but never came back.

Sometimes it's because another location offered a better incentive. More often, it's because that other location was simply **ready**, ready with information, approvals, and confidence.

Unreadiness shows up in subtle but damaging ways: incomplete site data, slow approvals, inconsistent messaging, infrastructure gaps, or community resistance born of surprise. Investors sense these gaps instantly. They may not say it, but they quietly cross you off the shortlist.

Investment readiness is therefore both an operational necessity and a competitive advantage.

The Three Layers of Readiness

1. Strategic Readiness – Knowing Where and Why

Strategic readiness is about understanding your investment priorities and aligning land, infrastructure, and policy to them.

Ask yourself:

- Do our zoning and land-use plans match our target sectors?
- Which precincts or corridors are best suited for future growth?

- Are we investing in the right infrastructure to support that growth?

If you're targeting advanced manufacturing, do you have industrial land with sufficient power, road access, and workforce proximity? If you're promoting agri-food investment, do you have access to logistics, water, and cold storage?

A simple **Investment Readiness Map** showing sites, services, and strategic priorities can align departments and partners and give investors a clear view of opportunity.

Strategic readiness means you're not reacting to proposals; you're shaping where they happen.

2. Operational Readiness – Knowing How

Operational readiness is about your internal systems: how you handle enquiries, manage data, and coordinate across departments.

It includes:

- a documented **investment enquiry process** from first contact to final decision;
- a shared **CRM** or database for tracking projects;
- clear **service standards** — for example, acknowledging enquiries within 24 hours and providing data within five business days;
- an internal **facilitation protocol** that defines roles for planning, engineering, environment, and economic development staff.

When staff know the process, investors feel it. Conversations are faster, information consistent, confidence higher.

Operational readiness also involves establishing clear lines of contact, with one empowered individual serving as the primary point to guide others through the system.

It's not about red tape; it's about reliability.

3. Community Readiness – Knowing Who and How Much

No investment succeeds without social licence. Community readiness means the groundwork has been done so residents, businesses, and local leaders understand the kind of investment being pursued and why.

That doesn't mean unanimous support for every project. It means open communication, early engagement, and consistent messaging about benefits and boundaries.

If you've already defined what types of investment your community wants (and doesn't want) (as discussed in Chapter 1) then community readiness becomes much easier. People know what to expect, and they trust that decisions align with shared values.

Councils that engage their communities early build resilience when challenging projects arise. Instead of reacting defensively, they can point back to agreed principles.

Social licence isn't a marketing campaign; it's a relationship built over time.

Defining and Testing Your Unique Value Proposition

Investment readiness isn't only about infrastructure and process, it's also about clarity of story.
A region can have perfect zoning, serviced land, and responsive systems, but if it can't clearly articulate **why** it stands out, investors will struggle to remember it.

That's where your **Unique Value Proposition (UVP)** comes in. It captures, in a few sentences, the essence of *why your place matters* in a crowded market.

A strong UVP answers three questions:

1. **Why here?** – What advantages does your region offer that others can't replicate?
2. **Why now?** – What makes this the right moment to invest?
3. **Why us?** – What makes your organisation credible, capable, and easy to work with?

These answers become the spine of your marketing, engagement, and partnerships.

Identifying Your Value Proposition

Start by taking inventory of your region's assets but don't stop there. Every region has land, lifestyle, and people; those are prerequisites, not differentiators.

Your value lies in the **specific intersections** between assets, industries, and ambitions. Ask:

- What can we do faster, cheaper, or more sustainably than others?
- Which industries already trust us with their operations?
- What stories prove our capability?
- What combinations make us distinctive is it logistics and lifestyle, research and renewables, scale and stability?

Look beyond hard assets. Your governance culture, partnership approach, and reliability are part of your value too. In an age where investors prize predictability, a region known for professionalism can be as attractive as one with a port or pipeline.

Testing with Target Audiences

Once you've drafted your UVP, **test it**. Don't rely solely on internal consensus; that often produces slogans that sound good locally but fall flat externally.

Share it with:

- existing investors — "Does this reflect your experience of doing business here?"
- prospective investors in target sectors;
- state-level agencies that pitch multiple regions;
- industry associations and chambers.

Listen carefully. Which phrases resonate? Which claims raise eyebrows? Which examples spark interest?

Testing forces honesty. If your message doesn't land, refine it until it does. The goal isn't to invent uniqueness, it's to **discover and articulate** it in language investors recognise.

Refining and Owning Your Message

A UVP is never static. As industries evolve and projects mature, your message should evolve too.
Maybe your region began as an affordable logistics hub but has since built strength in automation and advanced training make sure you update your story to reflect that.

Refine it annually, using real examples to strengthen credibility:

"Here, investors aren't just buying land, they're joining a region where renewable energy, skilled labour, and reliability intersect."

Once refined, **own it.** Embed your UVP everywhere: in council reports, social media, site tours, ministerial briefings. When every staff member can articulate the same clear message, your region sounds cohesive and confident, a place that knows who it is and why it matters.

From Message to Readiness

A compelling UVP doesn't just attract attention; it shapes priorities. When you know what your value proposition is, you can ensure that your infrastructure, land use, and policy decisions reinforce it.

If your story is about innovation, your planning and education partnerships should prove it. If your story is about sustainability, your energy choices should back it up.

Investment readiness, at its core, is alignment, between what you say, what you build, and what investors experience when they arrive.

Physical Readiness – Sites, Services and Infrastructure

1. Know Your Land and Assets

Investors often start with a simple question: *"What sites are available, and what's on them?"*

Create and maintain an **Investment Site Register** that includes:

- site size and ownership status;
- zoning and permitted uses;
- infrastructure availability (power, water, sewer, roads, broadband);
- distance to ports, airports, or markets;
- environmental constraints;
- photos, aerials, and maps.

Even approximate data, presented consistently, builds credibility. Work with property owners to ensure listings are genuine. Nothing frustrates investors more than discovering a promoted site isn't available.

Infrastructure Readiness

Hard infrastructure (energy, water, waste, digital, transport) underpins investment.

Know your capacities and constraints. Engage utilities early and keep communication open. Soft infrastructure matters too: skills, housing, childcare, health. Investors assess these when deciding where to locate people as well as projects.

An infrastructure gap analysis can highlight where investment is most viable now and where it will be soon.

Environmental and Regulatory Readiness

Know your flood zones, heritage areas, and biodiversity overlays. Maintain environmental data for priority sites, particularly brownfields. Transparency builds trust; surprises destroy it.

Frame constraints as challenges you've anticipated, not problems investors must uncover. Coordination between planning and environment teams ensures consistency and confidence.

Institutional Readiness – Systems, Speed and Certainty

Institutional readiness is about predictability. Investors can handle "no." What they can't handle is silence or contradiction.

Develop an **Investment Facilitation Charter** outlining:

- who to contact;

- what information will be provided;
- expected response times;
- escalation pathways;
- mutual responsibilities.

Make it public. A transparent process builds trust faster than any shortcut.

Readiness Through Partnerships

Readiness is shared. No council or agency can do it alone. Establish a **Readiness Taskforce** or **Investment Coordination Group** involving utilities, state agencies, developers, and education providers.

Regular meetings to share data and resolve bottlenecks build ownership and speed.

Partnership readiness also includes business and industry groups. Local firms that can supply, construct, or collaborate strengthen your investment story immeasurably.

Digital Readiness – The New Front Door

In today's world, your first impression is online. A professional, data-rich **Investment Portal** is essential. It should:

- present your UVP clearly;
- showcase sites, maps, and infrastructure;
- highlight success stories and testimonials;

- link to workforce, lifestyle, and housing information;
- make it easy to contact the right person (not a generic email or general number to call)

Treat your digital presence as your 24-hour front desk: always open, accurate, and welcoming.

Readiness as a Continuous Process

Markets, land, and expectations change. Conduct an **annual readiness review** covering:

- updated site and infrastructure data;
- staff capability;
- process checks;
- investor feedback;
- community sentiment.

Even a half-day internal workshop can identify improvements. Over time, readiness becomes muscle memory (a habit rather than a project).

Building Confidence Through Readiness

Readiness builds confidence. Confidence builds trust. Trust attracts investment.

When your team knows the system works, they exude calm professionalism. Investors sense it immediately. That confidence shortens decisions and creates momentum.

The most competitive regions aren't always the largest or richest; they're the ones that are prepared, coordinated, and credible.

A Final Reflection

Investment readiness is where preparation meets opportunity.

It's quiet work (spreadsheets, maps, meetings, process diagrams) but it's the work that determines whether your region is merely visible or genuinely competitive.

Being investment-ready means being ready to respond, ready to collaborate, and ready to deliver.

Because when the call comes, and it will, the difference between landing the project and watching it go elsewhere won't be luck. It will be readiness.

Chapter 8

Lead Generation and Prospecting

Building and Managing an Active Investor Pipeline

Every investment attraction program eventually faces the same question:

"Where do the investors actually come from?"

It's one thing to have a strong strategy, a well-prepared team, and ready-to-go sites but without a steady flow of leads, the engine stalls.

Lead generation is the heartbeat of investment attraction. It's the disciplined, ongoing process of identifying, engaging, and nurturing potential investors who match your region's priorities. Done well, it builds not just a pipeline of projects but a network of long-term relationships that sustain your region's growth for years.

The Purpose of Lead Generation

Lead generation is not about collecting as many names as possible. It's about connecting with the *right* prospects and to those whose needs align with your region's value proposition, capabilities, and ambitions.

A well-built pipeline allows you to:

- maintain consistent activity between major project announcements;
- test and refine your value proposition in real conversations;
- understand market sentiment in your target sectors;
- position your region as a credible option early in investors' decision processes.

Lead generation is both science and art, part data, part intuition, part relationship management.

Focus: The Difference Between Strategy and Scatter

Lead generation without focus is like fishing without bait, you may stay busy, but you won't catch much that matters.

Every conversation, email, and conference trip consumes time, budget, and mental energy. When those efforts aren't directed toward a clear target, the result is fatigue rather than traction.

Unfocused prospecting can lead to several problems:

- **Burnout of resources.** Teams spread themselves too thin, chasing dozens of low-quality leads instead of nurturing the few that really fit.
- **Weakened pitch.** Constantly shifting messages for different sectors and audiences makes your story sound generic rather than authentic.
- **Mixed community signals.** When a region seems to chase everything, it can appear opportunistic or inconsistent and lead to eroding local and investor confidence.

The most successful investment teams treat focus as an act of self-discipline. They know exactly what kind of investors they're looking for, and they spend most of their time there. They understand that every "no" to a poor-fit opportunity is a "yes" to something better aligned.

Focus doesn't mean ignoring unexpected opportunities, it means approaching them with awareness and proportional effort. If you're clear about your priorities, you can triage enquiries intelligently and manage the pipeline strategically rather than reactively.

In short: focus gives your lead generation momentum, structure, and sustainability. Without it, you risk exhaustion, confusion, and wasted potential.

The Investor Journey

Before generating leads, it helps to understand the path investors typically take:

1. **Awareness** – The investor becomes aware of your region through marketing, media, or networks.
2. **Interest** – They seek more information and make initial contact.
3. **Evaluation** – They assess sites, data, and conditions, comparing you with other locations.
4. **Engagement** – You begin detailed discussions and site visits.
5. **Commitment** – The project is confirmed and implemented.
6. **Aftercare** – The relationship continues, often leading to reinvestment.

Lead generation focuses on the first two stages **creating awareness** and **generating interest**, but it also sets the tone for everything that follows.

A professional first impression during prospecting builds trust that carries through to facilitation and aftercare.

Step 1: Define Your Target Audience

Lead generation starts with **clarity**, not activity. Before making a single phone call or attending a trade show, define *who* you want to attract.

Your targets should flow directly from your **focus sectors** and **value proposition**.

Ask:

- What types of companies align with our priority industries?

- What size and stage of business are we best suited to support — startups, mid-sized firms, or global leaders?
- Which countries or regions have existing trade or cultural ties with us?
- What supply chains already link to our local industries?

This targeting ensures every hour spent on outreach has purpose. It also prevents "scatter-gun" marketing that wastes money and confuses stakeholders.

If possible, build **target company profiles** which should be short summaries describing ideal investors by sector, scale, and motivation. For example:

"Mid-tier renewable energy developers seeking land with grid access within 100 km of transmission lines and strong council support for approvals."

Profiles like this help focus campaigns and brief partners clearly.

Step 2: Build Your Prospecting Toolkit

Lead generation relies on tools that help you find and manage opportunities systematically.

2.1 Data Sources

Use reliable databases and platforms to identify potential investors, such as:

- trade and industry directories;
- export and import databases;

- membership lists of chambers or peak bodies;
- event attendee lists;
- LinkedIn Sales Navigator or similar tools.

Combine data sources to build a manageable list of companies that meet your target profiles.

2.2 CRM System

All leads should be captured in a **Customer Relationship Management (CRM)** system. This is your institutional memory, it ensures relationships survive staff changes and allows you to track where each lead sits in the pipeline.

A basic CRM should record:

- company details and sector;
- contact information;
- source of the lead;
- stage in the pipeline;
- notes and next steps.

Consistent data entry is vital. A good CRM, well maintained, is worth more than any marketing campaign.

2.3 Marketing and Digital Assets

Ensure your digital presence supports your outreach. Prospects will visit your website, check your LinkedIn page, and search for media stories.

If your online content doesn't match your message, credibility evaporates before the conversation begins.

Step 3: Prospecting Channels

There are many ways to generate leads. The most effective programs use a mix that suits their scale and resources.

3.1 Direct Outreach

The simplest and most powerful form of prospecting is still the personal approach: email, phone call, or meeting.

Direct outreach works best when it's informed and relevant. Cold calls don't work; targeted introductions do.

For example:

"I noticed your company recently expanded into Southeast Asia and is seeking distribution capacity closer to Australian markets. We have available industrial land with direct highway and port access, could we discuss whether that fits your plans?"

3.2 Referrals and Networks

Existing investors, local businesses, accountants, and professional services firms can all be powerful referrers. People trust people they know.

Build a **referral network** by keeping these stakeholders informed of your focus sectors and the kind of investors you're seeking. Reward them with recognition, updates, and gratitude.

3.3 Events and Trade Missions

Industry events and trade missions can yield valuable leads, but only when approached strategically.

Before attending, set objectives:

- Which companies do you want to meet?
- What message will you deliver?
- How will you follow up afterwards?

A single well-prepared event can yield months of productive leads; an unplanned one yields a pile of forgotten business cards.

4. Digital Marketing and Content

High-quality online content attracts inbound leads. Articles, newsletters, case studies, and webinars that showcase your region's expertise build awareness among target audiences.

Use LinkedIn strategically, not for generic promotion, but to share practical insights that demonstrate credibility. Investors respond to substance, not slogans.

5. Partner Organisations

Collaborate with state and federal agencies, trade commissioners, and investment promotion partners. They often receive enquiries that can be referred your way but only if they understand what you offer and whom you want to attract.

Maintain open communication, provide updated information, and make it easy for them to promote your region confidently.

Step 4: Qualify and Prioritise Leads

Lead generation without qualification leads to exhaustion. Not every enquiry deserves equal effort.

Develop a simple **qualification matrix** to assess each lead against key criteria such as:

- **Strategic Fit** – Does it align with our priority sectors and community values?
- **Feasibility** – Does the company have financial and operational capacity?
- **Impact** – What potential jobs, supply-chain links, or diversification could it bring?
- **Readiness** – How serious and time-bound is the opportunity?
- **Risk** – Are there environmental, political, or reputational risks to consider?

Score each lead. Focus your energy where it delivers the most impact and communicate honestly with those that don't fit.

Investors appreciate clear expectations as much as they value speed.

Step 5: Nurture and Track Relationships

Investment attraction is rarely a one-off transaction. Many projects take 12–36 months to mature. Regular, professional follow-up keeps momentum alive.

Use your CRM to schedule check-ins, share updates, and record every interaction. Send relevant information new land-release updates, infrastructure announcements, or local success stories.

Think of your prospects as a *community*, not a list. The goal is to be present and helpful, not pushy. When they're ready to move, you'll be the first person they call.

Step 6: Evaluate and Refine

Refine your lead generation tactics continuously. Track which channels produce quality leads, and which don't.

Ask:

- Are most leads coming from one sector or source?
- What's our conversion rate from enquiry to project?
- Which types of outreaches yield genuine engagement?

Use data to adjust quarterly. Lead generation is not a campaign; it's a living system that gets smarter with time.

Common Mistakes to Avoid

1. **Confusing quantity with quality.** Ten well-researched leads are worth more than a hundred cold names.
2. **Neglecting follow-up.** Most opportunities are lost not from rejection but from silence.
3. **Ignoring focus.** Chasing too many sectors at once burns energy and weakens your narrative.

4. **Forgetting existing investors.** Some of your best new leads come from businesses already operating locally.

5. **Failing to close the loop internally.** If an enquiry reaches planning or utilities, ensure its tracked back into your CRM.

Turning Leads into Relationships

The best investment promoters understand that **every lead is a relationship in progress**.

Some will mature quickly, others may take years. Some may never convert but will still become advocates.

Treat every interaction as the start of a partnership. Keep promises, respond promptly, and offer insights, not just information. When investors realise you care about their success, not just your headline, trust builds and trust is what closes deals.

A Final Reflection

Lead generation without focus is like running a marathon in every direction.

When you know who you are, what you offer, and who you're trying to reach, every conversation has purpose. Your team's energy goes further, your story sounds sharper, and your reputation grows stronger.

Lead generation and prospecting aren't glamorous but they're the quiet work that fills the pipeline, builds relationships, and keeps your region's economic future in motion.

Because in the end, investment attraction isn't about chasing investors. It's about earning their confidence and having one focused, well-prepared conversation at a time.

Chapter 9

Investor Qualification and Assessment

Focusing Effort Where It Delivers the Most Impact

Not every investor is the right investor.

One of the hardest lessons for any investment promotion professional is that **activity is not the same as progress**. A full calendar doesn't always mean meaningful outcomes. Sometimes, it means your team is spending valuable time chasing opportunities that will never deliver. Not because the investors are bad people, but because the projects simply don't fit your region's strategy, capacity, or values.

That's why **qualification** sits at the heart of effective investment attraction. It's the discipline that converts ambition into efficiency, and efficiency into results.

The Purpose of Qualification

Investor qualification is the process of assessing an enquiry or lead to determine whether it's worth pursuing, and if so, at what level of effort.

Done well, it saves time, preserves energy, and strengthens credibility. It ensures your resources (time, money, political capital) are directed toward opportunities that have the best chance of success and the greatest community benefit.

Qualification doesn't mean saying "no" to everyone else; it means understanding *where* to say "yes" with intensity and *where* to engage more lightly.

Why Qualification Matters

Every investment office, no matter how large or small, faces the same challenge: **limited bandwidth**.
When resources are finite, prioritisation becomes survival. Without it, the result is exhaustion and frustration.

Unqualified leads drain time and morale. Staff spend hours preparing data for speculative or unrealistic proposals, while high-quality investors wait for responses. Councillors grow impatient, and the region's reputation suffers.

Qualification provides clarity and fairness. It gives your team a transparent way to explain (internally and externally) why certain projects receive more attention than others.

It also prevents what many practitioners call "political gravity" which is the tendency to chase high-profile projects that sound exciting but lack alignment or viability.

The Qualification Mindset

Qualification is as much about **mindset** as it is about systems.

It's the shift from "every enquiry is a potential win" to "every enquiry is a potential relationship to be managed strategically."

It's about curiosity before commitment and asking smart questions, not making quick promises.

Experienced investment officers know that a polite, well-reasoned "not a fit at this time" builds more long-term trust than an enthusiastic "yes" that later turns into silence or disappointment.

The Qualification Framework

An effective qualification process is built around a simple but disciplined framework.

Think of it as a funnel with three stages:

1. **Initial Screening** – Quick evaluation to identify genuine interest and eliminate poor fits.
2. **Detailed Assessment** – Deeper analysis of potential impact, feasibility, and alignment.
3. **Prioritisation and Action** – Deciding how much effort to invest, who leads engagement, and what support is appropriate.

This framework allows you to manage a wide range of enquiries without being overwhelmed.

Stage 1: Initial Screening – Filtering Early

The first screen should be fast, factual, and friendly. The goal is to gather enough information to understand whether the enquiry warrants deeper attention.

Ask basic but revealing questions:

- What exactly are you looking to invest in or build?
- What scale and timeframe are you considering?
- Have you identified potential sites or regions already?
- What are your infrastructure or workforce requirements?
- What stage are you in, is it early exploration or ready-to-commit?

If answers are vague, unrealistic, or inconsistent, that's a red flag. You can still respond courteously but avoid committing scarce resources too soon.

At this stage, you're assessing **credibility** and **fit**.

Stage 2: Detailed Assessment – Understanding Depth and Fit

For leads that pass the first screen, conduct a deeper assessment across five dimensions.

2.1 Strategic Fit

Does the project align with your focus sectors and community values?
Ask yourself:

- Does it contribute to long-term goals or fill a gap in the local economy?
- Does it strengthen existing supply chains or create new ones?
- Is it consistent with your sustainability, land use, and workforce strategies?

A project that fits strategically but lacks immediate feasibility might still warrant long-term engagement.

2.2 Economic Impact

Estimate the potential benefits:

- Capital investment value;
- Direct and indirect job creation;
- Supply-chain participation opportunities;
- Local expenditure during construction and operation.

Use consistent templates for estimating impacts so comparisons are fair.

2.3 Financial and Organisational Capacity

Assess whether the investor has the resources and track record to deliver.
Check:

- financial statements or public filings (if available);
- prior projects or operational footprint;
- reputation in the industry.

You're not conducting due diligence at this stage, you're just confirming basic credibility.

4. Readiness and Commitment

Is the project speculative or real?

- Have they secured financing or partners?
- Are they prepared to visit the site or engage local consultants?
- Have they identified key decision-makers?

Early commitment signals seriousness. Lack of clarity often means they're still shopping widely.

5. Risk and Reputation

Every project carries risk — such as environmental risks (like pollution or habitat disruption), social risks (such as community opposition or displacement), political risks (like regulatory changes or unstable government policies), or ethical risks (for example, conflicts of interest or questionable labour practices). These categories highlight the diverse challenges that can arise, making it essential to identify and manage each risk type proactively in your project documentation. By understanding these risks from the outset, you can implement strategies to mitigate potential issues and ensure your project aligns with community values and regulatory requirements.

Ask:

- Could this project damage community trust?
- Are there potential conflicts of interest or governance issues?
- Would the investor's reputation strengthen or weaken our region's brand?

Even financially sound projects can become liabilities if they generate local opposition or misalignment with community values.

Stage 3: Prioritisation and Action

Once you've assessed these factors, rank or score each project using a **Qualification Matrix**.

The Qualification Matrix

Criteria	High Priority (Score 3)	Medium (2)	Low (1)
Strategic Fit	Fully aligned with focus sectors and community vision	Partial alignment or adjacent sector	Limited or no alignment
Economic Impact	High-value investment and local job creation	Moderate benefit or niche market	Minimal measurable impact

Criteria	High Priority (Score 3)	Medium (2)	Low (1)
Financial Capacity	Proven, well-capitalised investor	Moderate capacity, needs partners	Unclear or unproven capability
Readiness	Project advanced, site visit planned	Early-stage exploration	Speculative or information-gathering only
Risk Profile	Low social/environmental risk, high reputation	Manageable risk	High risk or public concern likely

Total scores (out of 15) can be grouped as:

- **12–15:** *High priority* — proactive facilitation and senior engagement.
- **8–11:** *Moderate priority* — nurture and monitor, light-touch support.
- **Below 8:** *Low priority* — provide information and keep on file, but minimal resource allocation.

You can adapt the matrix to suit local contexts. Adding weighting for sustainability, Indigenous engagement, innovation potential, or other strategic priorities.

The key is consistency. When everyone uses the same system, prioritisation becomes defensible and transparent.

Managing Different Types of Investors

1. High-Value Strategic Investors

These are the game changers and are the large projects that align perfectly with your priorities and require close facilitation. Assign senior officers, coordinate multi-agency support, and brief political leaders early.

2. Emerging or Medium-Scale Investors

Promising but not yet transformative. Provide steady support, introduce local partners, and track progress. These often grow into your next big wins.

3. Opportunistic or Speculative Enquiries

Common in every region these are the early-stage proposals seeking free information or incentives. Respond courteously, provide general materials, and add them to your CRM for future follow-up.

4. Mismatched or High-Risk Projects

Politely decline or refer elsewhere. Protecting your credibility and community trust is more valuable than a short-term headline.

Transparency and Communication

Qualification isn't about closing doors but think about like it's about managing expectations.

When you decide not to prioritise an investor, communicate clearly and respectfully. A well-handled "no" can still lead to future opportunities.

For example:

"Thank you for considering our region. At present, our strategic priorities focus on renewable energy and advanced manufacturing. While your proposal doesn't align directly, we'd be happy to stay in touch and share updates as circumstances evolve."

That kind of response preserves relationships, reinforces professionalism, and keeps your reputation intact.

Using Qualification Data Strategically

Your qualification matrix shouldn't live in a spreadsheet that no one reads. Over time, it becomes a valuable data source for understanding patterns:

- Which sectors generate the most serious enquiries?
- Which types of projects most often stall or withdraw?
- How long does it take for qualified leads to convert?

This data helps refine focus sectors, adjust marketing strategies, and identify systemic barriers such as infrastructure constraints or policy gaps. In other words, qualification doesn't just help you manage leads; it helps you *learn from them.*

Balancing Focus with Flexibility

Qualification works best when paired with judgement. The matrix is a guide, not a gate.

A project that scores modestly might still be worth pursuing if it offers strategic visibility, innovation potential, or critical infrastructure. Conversely, a project that looks good on paper might be paused if community concerns are high or resources are stretched.

The key is balance and applying structure without losing intuition. Experienced practitioners know when to follow the rules and when to adapt.

Internal Alignment

Qualification only works if everyone agrees on the rules.

Make sure your councillors, executive team, and partners understand the framework.
Share examples of how projects are scored and prioritised. Transparency builds trust and avoids confusion when decisions are questioned later.

It also gives staff confidence and importantly they know they're working within a clear, fair system, not personal preference or politics.

A Final Reflection

Qualification is where professionalism meets discipline.

It's the quiet work that keeps investment attraction focused, credible, and sustainable. It protects your team from burnout, your region from poor-fit projects, and your reputation from overpromising.

When done well, qualification ensures that every hour spent on investor engagement is an hour invested wisely.

Because in the end, great investment attraction isn't about saying yes to everyone, it's about saying yes *to the right ones*, for the right reasons, at the right time.

That's how you move from being busy to being effective and from chasing projects to curating them.

Chapter 10

Facilitation and Site Selection Support

Turning Interest into Commitment

Once an investor is qualified and genuinely interested, the hard work and the real opportunity begins.

At this stage, your role shifts from **promoter** to **facilitator**. The tone of engagement changes: you're no longer just selling your region; you're helping the investor imagine their future there.

This is where deals are won or lost and not through glossy brochures or incentives, but through the quality, responsiveness, and confidence of your facilitation.

The most successful regions understand that investment attraction isn't about convincing; it's about **removing friction** and making it easy for investors to say "yes."

The Purpose of Facilitation

Facilitation is about turning interest into implementation. It's the set of actions that help investors navigate your systems, secure information, and move smoothly from consideration to decision.

A good facilitation process:

- **Reduces risk** by providing clarity and certainty;
- **Builds trust** through responsiveness and transparency;
- **Creates momentum** by coordinating approvals and stakeholders;
- **Shapes perception** — every interaction reflects how your region does business.

Facilitation is not about doing everything for the investor. It's about creating an environment where decisions can happen confidently and efficiently.

The "Concierge" Model of Investment Support

Think of facilitation like a concierge service.

A good concierge doesn't own the hotel; they don't cook the meals or clean the rooms. But they make the guest experience seamless by knowing who to call, what to arrange, and how to solve problems quickly.

In the same way, a skilled investment officer doesn't own the approvals or the land, but they know how to connect the investor with the right people, anticipate their needs, and ensure their experience feels supported, not bureaucratic.

Every minute saved, every confusion avoided, adds value.

The Investor Experience

From the investor's perspective, your region is one of many options. They are comparing not just sites and costs, but **ease of doing business**.

What they remember most isn't the data you provide, it's how you made them feel.

Did you respond quickly?
Did your information match your marketing claims?
Did your partners seem aligned or divided?
Did they feel confident you could deliver?

Investors are looking for reasons to trust. Facilitation is how you give them those reasons.

Preparing for Facilitation

Effective facilitation doesn't start when the investor calls, it starts long before.

The best teams invest time in preparation so they can move fast later. This includes:

- **Having your data ready.** Ensure key statistics (workforce, utilities, costs, demographics) are current and accessible.

- **Maintaining up-to-date site profiles.** Investors often request details within 24–48 hours; outdated maps or ownership information can kill momentum.
- **Knowing your internal pathways.** Map out who approves what, expected timeframes, and escalation contacts.
- **Pre-aligning key partners.** Ensure planning, infrastructure, utilities, and environmental officers understand the importance of responsiveness.

When everyone knows their role and the system runs smoothly, investors notice.

Step 1: Investor Onboarding

When an investor is qualified and ready to engage, start with a structured onboarding process.

Send a concise, professional email confirming:

- appreciation for their interest;
- your role as their primary contact;
- next steps (e.g., scheduling a meeting, providing data pack, arranging a visit);
- estimated response time for any requests.

This sets the tone: professional, predictable, and welcoming.

If the project is large or strategic, hold an **initial facilitation meeting** with internal stakeholders to brief them on the investor, project scope, and sensitivities. Early alignment prevents internal surprises later.

Step 2: Data Packs – Providing the Right Information

Investors make decisions based on information but the key is **relevance, not volume**.

Prepare **customised data packs** that focus on what the investor actually needs. Generic "regional profiles" are fine for awareness, but serious investors want detail.

A good data pack might include:

- overview of the region and key advantages (tailored to their sector);
- site options with maps, zoning, and servicing details;
- infrastructure and logistics access (ports, airports, highways, rail);
- workforce and training providers;
- utility availability and indicative pricing;
- relevant approvals processes and indicative timeframes;
- lifestyle and housing information for workforce relocation;
- contact points for government and industry partners.

Where possible, deliver it visually because investors process images and maps faster than text.

Avoid sending everything at once. Too much information can overwhelm. Curate what matters most and offer more detail on request.

Step 3: Site Selection Support

The **site visit** is often the defining moment in the investment journey. It's when the project stops being theoretical and becomes tangible.

A well-organised site visit can accelerate decision-making dramatically; a poorly managed one can undo months of goodwill.

Planning the Visit

- **Confirm objectives:** Ask what the investor wants to achieve — e.g., compare sites, meet officials, explore logistics.
- **Coordinate stakeholders:** Line up landowners, utilities, training providers, and local businesses relevant to their sector.
- **Prepare materials:** Maps, fact sheets, photographs, and case studies that reinforce your key messages.
- **Logistics:** Handle transport, catering, and scheduling smoothly — every detail communicates professionalism.

During the Visit

- Keep presentations brief and conversations focused.
- Use real people: engineers, business owners, training managers. Authenticity builds confidence.
- Showcase community pride, investors want to sense that locals value and support economic growth.

- Avoid overpromising. Transparency about challenges enhances credibility.

After the Visit

- Send a thank-you note within 24 hours.
- Provide any requested follow-up materials promptly.
- Record outcomes and next steps in your CRM.

A site visit is not an inspection, it's an audition. You're showing not just land, but the capability and culture of your place.

Step 4: Multi-Agency Coordination

Investment attraction is a team sport.

Large or complex projects often involve multiple agencies, planning, environment, transport, education, utilities, and sometimes state or federal partners.

As the facilitator, your role is to **coordinate**, not control. Ensure everyone understands:

- the project's scope and significance;
- the investor's expectations and timeframes;
- their own responsibilities and deadlines.

Regular check-ins and shared timelines prevent bottlenecks. Even if approvals take time, communication keeps confidence alive.

One of the most powerful phrases an investor can hear is:

"We've already spoken with our planning and infrastructure teams, and here's what the process will look like."

That single sentence signals competence and cohesion.

Step 5: Managing Expectations

Facilitation doesn't mean saying "yes" to everything. It means setting realistic expectations early and managing them carefully.

Be honest about timelines, costs, and limitations. Investors value predictability more than speed. A delayed project can be managed; a surprise cannot.

If something changes (a new regulation, cost escalation, or environmental concern) communicate it immediately. Silence breeds mistrust faster than bad news.

Transparency doesn't scare investors away; it draws the right ones closer.

Step 6: The Importance of Responsiveness

In investment attraction, **responsiveness is reputation**.

Even a short delay in response can send the wrong signal. Investors often interpret slow replies as slow systems.

Set internal standards for response times:

- Acknowledge all enquiries within one business day.
- Provide substantive responses within five days.
- Follow up if you're waiting on internal input, don't let requests disappear into inboxes.

Responsiveness is not about having all the answers instantly, it's about communicating progress.

Step 7: The Role of Leadership

Leadership visibility matters in facilitation.

When senior leaders (mayors, CEOs, directors) take time to meet investors, it signals seriousness and respect.
It also helps navigate sensitive issues quickly, especially where political or community confidence is needed.

However, leadership should be strategic, not performative. Bring them in when their presence adds weight or reassurance and not just for photos.

A good facilitation team knows when to deploy senior voices and when to protect them from early-stage distractions.

Step 8: Capturing and Sharing Lessons

Every facilitation experience teaches something about your processes, your readiness, or your team.

After major projects or site visits, hold a **debrief**:

- What went well?
- Where did we lose time or clarity?
- What could we improve next time?

Record lessons in your CRM or internal guidebook. Over time, you'll build a playbook tailored to your region's strengths and quirks.

Continuous learning turns facilitation from an event into an evolving capability.

Common Pitfalls in Facilitation

1. **Overpromising and underdelivering.**
   Nothing erodes trust faster than enthusiasm that turns into silence.
2. **Information overload.**
   Investors need clarity, not clutter. Focus on relevance.
3. **Internal silos.**
   Poor coordination between departments creates delays and mixed messages.
4. **Ignoring the small stuff.**
   A missed airport pickup, or outdated map may seem trivial but investors notice.
5. **Neglecting follow-up.**
   The days after a visit are when impressions solidify. Respond fast and follow through.

Facilitation and Focus

Facilitation, like lead generation, benefits from focus.

When you're clear about your region's priorities, you can deliver support efficiently. You know which projects deserve full coordination and which require only light-touch service.

Without focus, every enquiry risks becoming an all-hands exercise. Teams burn out chasing every possibility, losing sight of strategic priorities.

Focused facilitation ensures your best energy goes to projects that truly fit protecting both your staff and your reputation.

A Final Reflection

Facilitation is where investment attraction becomes tangible. It's the quiet, coordinated effort that turns conversations into commitments.

It's not glamorous work and most of it happens in emails, meetings, and logistics checklists, but it's the work that defines whether investors leave saying, *"They were organised, efficient, and trustworthy."*

That perception travels faster than any marketing campaign.

Because when investors feel that you're on their side (solving problems, anticipating needs, and following through) remember they don't just choose your region.
They become your advocates.

That's when investment attraction stops being transactional and becomes relational and relationships are what build economies that last.

Chapter 11

Designing and Delivering Incentives

Using Incentives Strategically — Not Desperately

Few topics in investment attraction spark as much debate as incentives.

For some, they're a vital competitive tool that acts as the lever that tips a project across the line. For others, they're a race to the bottom and a costly contest where regions give away too much for too little.

The truth lies somewhere in between.

Incentives can be powerful when they're **strategic, transparent, and targeted**.

They can also be destructive when they're reactive, secretive, or misaligned with community goals.

The purpose of this chapter is to help you design and deliver incentives that *reinforce* your strategy rather than undermine it.

What Incentives Are and What They Aren't

An incentive is any **advantage or facilitation** offered to reduce investor risk or cost, making your region more attractive for a project that delivers public benefit.

They can be:

- **Financial** – grants, rate relief, rebates, or infrastructure contributions.
- **Non-financial** – fast-tracked approvals, workforce training, data access, introductions to local partners.

But incentives are **not substitutes for competitiveness**. They should complement your strengths, not compensate for weaknesses.

If you find yourself offering large incentives simply to "stay in the race," it's time to revisit your value proposition. Incentives work best when they amplify what already makes your region compelling.

Why Regions Offer Incentives

Every incentive should have a **purpose beyond the project itself**.

Well-designed incentives can:

- accelerate investment decisions;
- stimulate development in priority sectors or locations;
- encourage innovation, sustainability, or local procurement;
- strengthen workforce capability through training partnerships;
- unlock co-investment from the private sector or higher levels of government.

When incentives are used strategically, they're not handouts. They're *investments in outcomes* that align with your community's vision.

The Risks of Poorly Designed Incentives

Used without discipline, incentives can backfire.

Common pitfalls include:

- **Overbidding** – offering more than necessary for a project that would have come anyway.
- **Opacity** – deals made without transparency, damaging public trust.
- **Short-termism** – rewarding activity rather than long-term impact.
- **Misalignment** – subsidising sectors that don't fit community goals.
- **Dependency** – creating expectations that every future investor deserves similar treatment.

The antidote is governance, evidence, and consistency.

The Golden Rule: Incentives Follow Strategy

Incentives should never lead strategy, they should follow it.

If your focus sectors and value proposition are clear, incentives should **support those priorities**, not override them.

Ask three questions before offering any incentive:

1. **Does this project align with our focus sectors and community values?**
2. **Would the project proceed without this support?**
3. **What measurable public benefit will result and how will we verify it?**

If the answers are unclear, pause.
An incentive without alignment is just a cost.

Incentives Aren't Always the Deal Breaker

It's easy to assume that the regions offering the biggest incentives always win.
But in reality, most investors make decisions based on a mix of **value, confidence, and relationships** (not just subsidies).

For serious investors, incentives are rarely the deal breaker.
They're the *cherry on top*, not the cake itself.

What carries far more weight is the overall **investment experience**:

- a clear and credible **Unique Value Proposition** that differentiates your region;
- a **coordinated, responsive team** that knows its processes and partners;
- **access to decision-makers** who can provide clarity quickly; and
- a genuine **willingness to help**. The human element that gives investors' confidence they'll be supported long after the ribbon-cutting.

Investors talk about *friction costs* which are the delays, uncertainty, or confusion that slow decisions. A polished UVP, backed by professional facilitation, often reduces those friction costs far more effectively than any financial incentive.

In short, incentives may help close a deal, but **they rarely open the door**.
A credible story, a prepared region, and a committed team are what bring investors through it.

Types of Incentives

1. Financial Incentives

These are the most visible and often the most politically sensitive.

Common forms include:

- **Rate or tax relief:** temporary reduction or deferral to support establishment.
- **Infrastructure contributions:** shared funding for roads, utilities, or site preparation.
- **Direct grants or rebates:** tied to job creation, training, or capital-investment thresholds.
- **Land discounts or lease incentives:** providing sites below market rate for strategic projects.

When used, financial incentives should always be:

- **time-bound** (not permanent);
- **conditional** (linked to performance);
- **transparent** (subject to reporting);
- **benchmarked** (so they don't distort the market).

2. Non-Financial Incentives

Often overlooked, non-financial incentives can be just as powerful:

- **Fast-tracked approvals and dedicated facilitation teams.**
- **Access to government or industry networks.**
- **Tailored workforce training through local RTOs or TAFEs.**
- **Assistance with housing or relocation for key staff.**
- **Marketing and visibility support (case studies or co-branding).**

These forms of support are lower-cost and often more meaningful to investors who prize certainty over subsidy.

Designing an Incentive Framework

A good framework creates clarity before you need it. It defines eligibility and provides a transparent process, ensuring consistency across projects and protection against political pressure.

1. Guiding Principles

Adopt principles such as:

- Alignment with strategic sectors and community values.
- Demonstrable public benefit.
- Performance-based and time-limited.
- No unfair competition with existing businesses.
- Transparent governance and reporting.

2. Governance Structure

Establish clear roles and thresholds:

- **Operational team:** analysis and recommendations.
- **Executive or council:** approval for major incentives.
- **Audit or oversight body:** monitors compliance and outcomes.

3. Assessment Criteria

Assess every proposal for:

- strategic alignment;
- economic and fiscal impact;
- community and sustainability benefit;
- risk exposure.

Consistency avoids ad-hoc decisions.

Linking Incentives to Measurable Outcomes

Every incentive should include clear **performance conditions** and consequences for non-performance.

Typical conditions:

- jobs created within a defined timeframe;
- minimum capital investment;
- evidence of local procurement or training;
- sustainability commitments.

If milestones aren't met, incentives can be reduced, deferred, or withdrawn.
Accountability ensures public value equals public investment.

The Importance of Transparency

Transparency is the currency of credibility.

Communities deserve to know how resources are used and what benefits they deliver. Secrecy breeds suspicion.

Publish an **Incentive Register** or annual summary showing:

- total incentive values (aggregated where confidentiality applies);
- expected vs actual outcomes;
- supported sectors;
- lessons learned.

Transparency reassures both the public and future investors that your system is principled, not political.

Incentives and Community Perception

Every incentive tells a story.

Handled poorly, it can spark headlines about "corporate welfare."
Handled well, it demonstrates leadership and partnership.

Communicate openly about *why* an incentive was offered and *what* it delivers. Link it to community priorities like jobs, innovation, sustainability, or regional renewal.

When people see alignment with their own values, support follows.

Encouraging Non-Financial Partnerships

Some of the most effective "incentives" don't involve money.

Investors consistently cite **ease of doing business**, **local cooperation**, and **speed of decision-making** as decisive factors.

Offer:

- a single point of contact;
- introductions to suppliers and training providers;
- marketing visibility through council or regional channels;
- access to workforce programs.

These low-cost actions communicate something powerful: *we want your investment to succeed, not just arrive.*

Balancing Flexibility and Fairness

Frameworks must balance **flexibility** and **fairness**.

A rigid system deters good projects; a loose one invites inconsistency.

Use tiered approval levels, small incentives under delegation, larger ones by council or board. Flexibility with structure is the hallmark of maturity.

Incentives and Focus

Incentives, like lead generation and facilitation, work best when your **focus** is clear.

When you know your target sectors, you can design incentives that speak directly to them:

- Renewable-energy zones → infrastructure co-investment.

- Advanced manufacturing → training and innovation partnerships.
- Tourism or creative industries → marketing and streamlined approvals.

Without focus, incentives become scattergun; with focus, they become precision tools that shape your economy with intent.

Avoiding the “Incentive Trap”

Investors may hint that other regions are offering bigger packages. This is where leadership matters.

Before matching an offer, ask:

- Does the project truly need the incentive?
- Is the opportunity unique enough to justify it?
- What precedent will it set?

Investors respect professionalism. If you hold your line and explain your framework confidently, they’ll often appreciate the clarity even if the answer is “no.”

Never outbid your value proposition. If a deal depends solely on incentives, it’s not the right deal.

Evaluating Incentive Performance

Post-implementation evaluation is essential.

Within 12–24 months of completion, review:

- Were promised outcomes achieved?

- What was the cost-benefit ratio?
- Were there unintended effects?
- How did the community perceive it?

Publish key findings and feed lessons back into the framework. Over time, this builds institutional memory and accountability.

A Final Reflection

Incentives are tools, not trophies.

Used wisely, they accelerate the right kind of investment and the projects that bring jobs, innovation, and resilience. Used poorly, they erode trust and weaken competitiveness.

The difference lies in **intention and discipline**.

When incentives are tied to strategy, governed transparently, and evaluated honestly, they become instruments of leadership. Helping your region compete not by paying more, but by *standing for more*.

Because in the end, the most attractive incentive you can offer isn't a grant or a rebate.
It's the confidence investors feel when they know they're entering a place that's prepared, principled, and proud of what it stands for.

Chapter 12

Aftercare: Where the Real Investment Happens

Turning One-Time Projects into Long-Term Partnerships

In economic development, it's easy to celebrate ribbon-cuttings and announcements. New projects make headlines, generate political capital, and signal progress.

But the real work and the real value often begins after the cameras are gone.

That's the realm of **aftercare**: the quiet, deliberate process of supporting investors once they've landed, helping them embed in the community, solve problems, and grow with confidence.

Aftercare isn't an optional extra. It's the foundation of sustainable investment attraction. Because when investors succeed, they reinvest and they tell others about it.

Why Aftercare Matters

Studies consistently show that **up to 70% of new jobs and investment** in most regions come from existing investors expanding their operations and not from new arrivals.

These are the companies that already know your workforce, suppliers, and systems. They've built trust, learned how to navigate local processes, and often developed deep community ties.

When they expand, it's a signal to others that your region delivers on its promises.

Aftercare turns initial projects into *platforms for further growth*. It's also one of the most cost-effective economic development strategies you can invest in. Far cheaper than finding, courting, and landing brand-new investors.

The Three Goals of Aftercare

A good aftercare program aims to:

1. **Retain** – Keep existing investors confident, engaged, and operationally successful.
2. **Grow** – Help them expand, innovate, or diversify within the region.
3. **Advocate** – Turn them into ambassadors who promote your place to peers and partners.

Each goal builds on the last. Retention creates stability; growth builds capacity; advocacy multiplies visibility.

Aftercare as Relationship Management

At its core, aftercare is about **relationships** ones that are consistent, authentic, and professional relationships that build trust over time.

Investors are no different from local businesses: they want to feel heard, supported, and valued. When problems arise (a planning issue, a skills gap, a regulatory change) they should know exactly who to call, and they should trust that the call will be answered.

Good aftercare teams operate like relationship managers. They don't wait for issues to surface; they check in proactively, listen, and connect investors to the right people before challenges become crises.

The Aftercare Lifecycle

Aftercare follows a simple lifecycle that mirrors the investor's journey:

1. **Onboarding and Integration** – Helping new investors establish operations smoothly.
2. **Monitoring and Support** – Checking in regularly to identify needs or barriers.
3. **Growth and Expansion** – Supporting reinvestment or scaling activity.

4. **Retention and Advocacy** – Strengthening loyalty and capturing success stories.

Each stage deepens engagement and turns transactional relationships into partnerships.

Step 1: Onboarding and Integration

Aftercare starts the day the deal is signed and not six months later when the investor runs into problems.

The onboarding phase sets the tone for everything that follows. It's about making sure the transition from decision to delivery is smooth.

Actions might include:

- assigning a dedicated liaison or account manager;
- coordinating introductions to local suppliers, training providers, and community networks;
- providing clear information about approvals, permits, and local services;
- helping new employees integrate into the community (housing, schools, lifestyle support).

When onboarding is handled well, investors feel supported, not abandoned. When it's ignored, they start second-guessing their decision.

Step 2: Monitoring and Support

Once operations are up and running, maintain regular contact and not to "check up," but to stay connected.

A quarterly or biannual check-in, framed around value rather than bureaucracy, can make a huge difference.

Questions to ask might include:

- How are things going with your operations and workforce?
- Are there any upcoming plans we should know about?
- Are you facing challenges where we might be able to assist?
- Are there suppliers, skills, or partnerships you'd like to connect with locally?

Keep notes in your CRM. Over time, these small interactions paint a powerful picture of your region's business climate to what's working, what's not, and where support is most needed.

Step 3: Growth and Expansion

This is where aftercare delivers its biggest return.

Expansion investment is often the easiest and most rewarding kind because the trust, processes, and track record already exist. But it rarely happens automatically.

Many investors need reassurance before committing additional capital: reassurance that the region still fits their long-term plans, that approvals remain predictable, that skilled labour and infrastructure will be there as they scale.

This is where your proactive engagement pays off. By understanding investors' growth plans early, you can anticipate their needs by helping them pilot new ideas, expand facilities, or trial new technologies.

Pilot and Scale: Different Risk Appetites

Not every investor grows in the same way.

Some prefer to **start small**, piloting a concept, testing workforce capacity, or assessing logistics before scaling up. Others arrive **"all in"** and are confident in their model and ready to establish large-scale operations from day one.

Both approaches are valid, but they require different facilitation styles:

- For **pilot-style investors**, focus on flexibility and feedback. Help them learn fast and remove early frictions so their proof-of-concept succeeds. If the pilot works, scaling usually follows naturally.
- For **all-in investors**, focus on certainty and execution. They've already made the leap, and your job is to deliver stability, manage risk, and ensure the region meets its promises.

Understanding an investor's risk appetite early allows you to tailor your support and pace your engagement accordingly.

Supporting Expansion Proactively

Some practical ways to support growth include:

- alerting investors to new funding or partnership opportunities;
- facilitating expansion approvals and site access;
- coordinating workforce or training support;

- connecting them to export programs or innovation initiatives;
- promoting their success through case studies and media.

The message you're sending is simple: *We don't just want you to invest here, we want you to thrive here.*

Step 4: Retention and Advocacy

When investors feel supported and valued, they become powerful ambassadors. They'll speak positively about your region in industry networks, attract their suppliers to co-locate, and influence future investors' perceptions.

Encourage advocacy by:

- showcasing investor success stories in newsletters, case studies, and events;
- inviting them to participate in advisory groups or economic development forums;
- asking for testimonials or referrals when appropriate.

A respected local investor's endorsement often carries more weight than any marketing campaign. Advocacy also strengthens community trust and helps locals see tangible, ongoing benefits from investment rather than one-off announcements.

Common Challenges in Aftercare

1. **Neglect after the win.**
   Too often, once a project is landed, attention shifts to

the next one. Relationships fade, small problems grow, and opportunities for expansion are missed. This can often happen to state or federal led investment.

2. **Lack of structure.**
   Aftercare can't rely solely on personalities. It needs systems which includes a contact schedule, CRM records, and defined account managers.

3. **Reactive support.**
   Waiting for investors to reach out usually means you're already behind. Proactivity builds trust and prevents escalation.

4. **Staff turnover.**
   If relationships live only in individual inboxes, continuity is lost. Institutionalise relationships so transitions are smooth.

5. **Underestimating the soft stuff.**
   Sometimes what investors value most isn't a grant or approval, it's being invited to local events, connected with schools, or included in community life.

Building an Aftercare Framework

A structured approach helps embed aftercare across your organisation.

1. **Mapping and Segmentation**

   List all active investors and segment them by size, sector, and strategic importance. High-impact or high-visibility investors might warrant quarterly contact; smaller ones perhaps twice a year.

2. **Assigning Responsibility**
   Each major investor should have a dedicated relationship manager. Someone they know by name and can contact directly.
3. **Tracking and Reporting**

   Use your CRM to log contact dates, discussion notes, issues raised, and outcomes. Regular reporting helps identify trends or emerging issues.
4. **Integration with Business Support**
   Align aftercare with your local business support programs (grants, training, export assistance). Many investors' needs mirror those of domestic firms.

Aftercare and Focus

Aftercare, like attraction, benefits from focus.

You can't give every investor equal attention and nor should you. Prioritise those that:

- have significant economic impact or growth potential;
- align with target sectors;
- act as flagship employers or advocates.

That doesn't mean ignoring smaller businesses it just means managing effort proportionally and strategically. Focused aftercare ensures your limited resources deliver maximum impact.

Measuring Aftercare Success

Aftercare success can be tracked through:

- investor satisfaction surveys;
- number of reinvestment or expansion projects;
- issues resolved through facilitation;
- advocacy participation (case studies, referrals);
- retention rates of key investors over time.

Combine quantitative metrics with qualitative stories. The best evidence of success is when investors themselves tell others, *"This is a great place to do business."*

A Final Reflection

Aftercare is the heartbeat of sustainable economic development. It's the quiet, relationship-driven work that builds confidence, loyalty, and legacy. When investors feel supported, they stay. When they see others expanding successfully, they invest again.

Some will start small by testing, piloting, learning before scaling. Others will arrive with bold ambition and big commitments. Both deserve a system that's ready, responsive, and reliable.

Because the goal of investment attraction isn't just to land new names on a list. It's to create a community of investors who believe in your place and who grow with you, speak for you, and stay for the long term. That's when investment stops being a transaction and becomes a relationship and relationships are what prosperity is built on.

Chapter 13

Working with Partners and Allies

Building the Ecosystem That Makes Investment Work

Investment attraction is a team sport.

No single organisation, not even the most capable investment promotion office can do it alone. Success depends on a network of partners who share information, align priorities, and deliver a consistent experience to investors. This is the essence of *collaborative competitiveness* and the idea that regions compete best when they cooperate internally.

Whether you're a local council, regional development organisation, or state agency, your ability to attract and retain investment will always depend on the strength of your partnerships.

Why Partnerships Matter

Partnerships expand your reach, deepen your capability, and build credibility.

They provide:

- **Data and insight** – access to the latest trends, workforce figures, and infrastructure plans.
- **Specialised expertise** – technical, regulatory, or sectoral knowledge you may not hold in-house.
- **Delivery capacity** – the ability to move projects faster through coordinated effort.
- **Collective reputation** – investors gain confidence when they see multiple agencies working seamlessly together.

When partners trust each other, they can focus on solving problems rather than negotiating territory.

The Partnership Mindset

Effective collaboration begins with mindset.

It's about shifting from *ownership* to *outcomes*. From *protecting turf* to *sharing success*.
From *transactional relationships* to *trusted alliances*.

Partnerships thrive on three qualities: **clarity, reciprocity, and respect**.

- **Clarity** means everyone understands roles, responsibilities, and boundaries.

- **Reciprocity** means giving as much as you receive and not forgetting to share credit, data, and visibility.
- **Respect** means valuing the different strengths that each partner brings.

When those principles are in place, collaboration becomes not just possible, but powerful.

Mapping Your Partnership Ecosystem

Every region has a web of potential allies. The key is to know who they are and how they fit.

Your ecosystem might include:

1. Government Partners

- **State and Federal Agencies:** For funding, infrastructure coordination, and policy alignment.
- **Regional Development Organisations:** For broader geographic promotion and shared marketing.
- **Other Councils:** For cross-boundary projects or shared precincts.

2. Industry and Business Networks

- **Chambers of Commerce, Industry Groups, and Peak Bodies:** For sector insights and introductions.
- **Anchor Companies:** Major employers or investors who can advocate for the region.

- **Professional Services Firms:** Accountants, engineers, real estate agents, lawyers are often first contact points for investors.

3. Education and Training Institutions

- **Universities, TAFEs, and RTOs:** For workforce development, R&D, and innovation partnerships.
- **Schools and Careers Programs:** For future skills pipelines.

4. Infrastructure and Utilities

- **Energy, Water, Waste, and Telecommunications Providers:** For feasibility and servicing data.
- **Transport and Logistics Partners:** Airports, ports, and freight networks.

5. Community and Social Partners

- **Traditional Owners and Indigenous Organisations:** For cultural engagement and land-use collaboration.
- **Community Organisations and NGOs:** For workforce participation, housing, and inclusion programs.

Mapping this ecosystem (even in a simple diagram) helps identify who needs to be involved at each stage of the investment process.

Coordination, Not Competition

It's natural for agencies or councils to feel competitive, especially when funding, headlines, or recognition are on the line. But competition within a region often confuses investors and weakens everyone's credibility.

Investors don't want to navigate politics; they want to see partnership. The most successful regions project **unity of purpose**. They might have multiple players, but they speak with one voice. This doesn't mean every organisation has the same role. It means they're aligned on message and process. When investors receive consistent information from all levels of government, their confidence multiplies.

Partner Roles Through the Investment Lifecycle

1. Attraction

- Coordinate marketing and outreach with state or regional partners.
- Align target sectors and messaging to avoid duplication.
- Share prospect information (with confidentiality protocols) to strengthen regional pitches.

2. Facilitation

- Involve relevant agencies early (planning, infrastructure, environment, and utilities).
- Designate a lead contact or "case manager" who coordinates internally and externally.
- Keep communication transparent to avoid mixed messages.

3. Aftercare and Expansion

- Share aftercare responsibilities with partners.
- Regularly convene investor roundtables or business councils to identify barriers to reinvestment.
- Coordinate advocacy and visibility efforts for expanding companies.

When each partner knows their role, facilitation becomes smoother, faster, and more credible.

Building Effective Communication Channels

Strong partnerships require intentional communication.

Establish formal mechanisms such as:

- **Regular coordination meetings** (monthly or quarterly) between key agencies.
- **Shared project tracking systems** or dashboards to monitor progress.
- **Joint briefings or updates** to councillors, boards, or ministers.
- **Crisis or escalation protocols** to resolve bottlenecks quickly.

Informal relationships matter too, that means coffee catchups, quick phone calls, mutual updates. Trust often grows in the small moments between meetings.

Aligning Data and Messaging

One of the most common frustrations for investors is receiving different answers from different agencies.

To avoid this, align your data and messaging across partners.

- Agree on consistent population, workforce, and infrastructure statistics.
- Maintain a shared library of approved facts, maps, and infographics.
- Coordinate media and marketing so language and tone are consistent.

Even minor inconsistencies like two different job numbers for the same project can erode confidence. Consistency signals competence.

Joint Marketing and Promotion

When done strategically, joint marketing amplifies everyone's reach.

Examples include:

- **Regional Investment Collateral:** Shared brochures or digital portals showcasing multiple councils or zones.
- **Joint Trade Missions:** Presenting a united regional presence at international events.
- **Themed Campaigns:** For example, "Invest in Queensland's Energy Corridor" or "Australia's Smart Food Belt."

Collaborative marketing tells a stronger story, one of scale, connectivity, and cooperation. Just ensure partners agree upfront on branding, messaging, and leads management to avoid confusion later.

Sharing Credit and Success

In collaborative work, credit must be shared generously. If your region wins an investment through collective effort, acknowledge every partner's role publicly and privately. Investors notice humility and professionalism. Shared recognition will build trust and ensures others will want to work with you again.

The goal isn't individual glory; it's regional reputation.

Partnering with Education and Training Providers

Workforce development is one of the most critical areas for collaboration.

By partnering with universities, TAFEs, and training organisations, you can:

- align courses with local industry needs;
- create customised training programs for new investors;
- support internships and apprenticeships that connect students to employers;
- foster research and development partnerships that drive innovation.

When education and industry move together, investors gain confidence that skills pipelines will meet future demand.

Working with State and Federal Agencies

State and federal agencies often have broader networks, funding programs, and international reach.

Engage them early:

- Share information about your region's target sectors, available sites, and investment priorities.
- Keep them updated on major leads or facilitation projects.
- Seek their input on policy, infrastructure, or grants that could support investors.

A strong relationship with your state investment agency or trade office can multiply your visibility internationally. But remember, partnership goes both ways. Make it easy for them to promote your region by providing clear, accurate, and timely information (avoid the 60-page prospectus).

Engaging the Private Sector

The private sector is not just a recipient of investment, it's a partner in attracting it.

Local companies, developers, and professional service providers can be powerful advocates. They interact daily with potential investors and can offer on-the-ground insights that government can't.

Create opportunities for collaboration such as:

- **Investor Advisory Panels or Roundtables** – regular forums for business leaders to share trends and feedback.
- **Supply-Chain Mapping Projects** – highlighting local capabilities that strengthen investment cases.
- **Co-marketing Initiatives** – featuring business success stories that showcase regional competitiveness.

Private-sector partners bring credibility because they speak from experience, not policy.

Building Trust Over Time

Partnerships succeed at the speed of trust.

Trust is built when:

- partners follow through on commitments;
- communication is open and honest;
- successes are shared and failures owned collectively.

Trust allows tough conversations to happen without defensiveness. It also makes collaboration more resilient when political or leadership changes occur because the relationships extend beyond individuals.

Measuring and Celebrating Collaboration

Like everything in economic development, partnerships should be measured and celebrated.

Track and report:

- number of joint projects facilitated;
- co-funded initiatives delivered;
- shared marketing campaigns completed;
- partner satisfaction through feedback surveys.

Celebrate wins publicly. Host partner appreciation events or highlight collaborations in newsletters and reports. Recognition keeps motivation high and relationships warm.

A Final Reflection

Partnerships play a fundamental role in attracting investment, providing the framework necessary for the development of ideas, projects, and opportunities. When partners operate with mutual trust, strategic planning is integrated with infrastructure, state agencies share valuable leads, and educational institutions tailor training to current needs, the overall system functions efficiently. This environment is immediately apparent to investors.

Collaboration not only enhances capability but also increases credibility. In an investment landscape where reliability and strong relationships are essential, being recognised as a region that consistently demonstrates effective cooperation can serve as a significant competitive advantage.

Chapter 14

The Changing Nature of Investment

Adapting to a World in Transition

The world of investment is changing faster than at any point in recent history.

What once defined competitiveness with cheap land, low labour costs, and basic infrastructure, is no longer enough. Today, investors weigh digital capability, supply-chain resilience, renewable energy access, community reputation, and political stability just as heavily as cost.

For local governments and investment professionals, the message is clear: **the fundamentals of place-making remain the same, but the rules of attraction have changed.**

The New Investment Landscape

Over the past decade, global shocks have rewritten the map of economic opportunity.

- **The pandemic** exposed fragile supply chains and the dangers of over-concentration in single markets.
- **Geopolitical tensions** — from trade wars and tariffs to regional conflicts and they have reshaped flows of goods, capital, and talent.
- **The energy transition** has moved from theory to necessity, driving unprecedented investment in renewables, critical minerals, and low-carbon industries.
- **Digitalisation and AI** are transforming how companies operate, where they locate, and what skills they need.
- **Demographic shifts** — ageing workforces in some countries, youth bulges in others, are redefining where talent will come from.

Together, these forces are not just influencing individual projects; they're changing the very logic of global investment.

1. Digital Transformation and Artificial Intelligence

Digital technology is now the backbone of almost every industry. Data centres, automation, robotics, and AI are creating entirely new location factors.

Investors increasingly seek regions that offer:

- **reliable high-speed connectivity**;
- **digital skills and data literacy**;
- **cyber-security frameworks**;
- **innovation ecosystems** that link business, research, and government.

Artificial Intelligence is reshaping investment in three ways:

1. **Smarter Site Selection:** Companies use AI-driven analytics to compare regions instantly on hundreds of variables like workforce, logistics, costs, and even community sentiment.
   Regions that manage and present their data well are far more likely to appear on those digital shortlists.
2. **Automation and Productivity:** As automation reduces labour intensity, proximity to workforce becomes less about numbers and more about *skills*. This favours regions with strong training systems and lifelong learning cultures.
3. **Digital Infrastructure as Core Infrastructure:** High-capacity broadband, data storage, and energy-efficient computing are now as critical as roads and ports. Regions that treat digital networks as public infrastructure, not luxury services, will stay ahead.

For investment professionals, the challenge is to integrate digital readiness into every pitch and demonstrating that their region can support both human and machine intelligence.

2. The Rise of Renewable Energy and Decarbonisation

The global race toward net-zero emissions is transforming capital flows. Trillions of dollars are being redirected into **renewable energy, battery storage, hydrogen, circular manufacturing, and clean transport**.

Companies across sectors are under pressure from investors, customers, and regulators to reduce carbon intensity. They are choosing locations that help them meet sustainability goals and places with:

- abundant renewable power and green hydrogen potential;
- supportive regulatory frameworks;
- access to critical minerals and recycling capabilities;
- credible climate adaptation and resilience planning.

Regions that can provide *clean, reliable, and affordable energy* are now magnets for advanced manufacturing, data centres, and resource processing.

Conversely, regions dependent on fossil-fuel infrastructure must manage transition carefully and investing in workforce reskilling, new industry clusters, and community adaptation.

For practitioners, the takeaway is simple: **renewable advantage can be a competitive advantage.**

3. Geopolitics, Supply-Chain Security, and Tariffs

Geopolitics has re-entered the investment equation in a way not seen for decades.

The era of hyper-globalisation, where production chased the lowest cost anywhere in the world is giving way to **"friend-shoring" and "near-shoring."**

Companies are reassessing where and with whom they do business, prioritising:

- political stability;
- rule of law and transparent governance;
- secure and diversified supply chains;
- proximity to trusted trading partners.

Trade tensions between major economies, new tariff regimes, and restrictions on sensitive technologies (like semiconductors and critical minerals) have made reliability more valuable than cost alone.

This shift creates both challenges and opportunities for regions like Australia.
As a trusted democracy with strong institutions, Australia is seen as a **safe haven for capital** but safety alone isn't enough. Investors still demand speed, certainty, and capability.

Local and regional practitioners can capitalise on this environment by positioning their regions as *secure, stable, and connected bases* for companies looking to hedge against global uncertainty.

4. Demographics and the Global War for Talent

Investment follows talent.

While technology can automate tasks, it can't replace creativity, problem-solving, and collaboration which are the human skills that drive innovation.

However, the global workforce is changing dramatically:

- Many advanced economies face **ageing populations** and shrinking labour pools.
- Emerging economies have **youth bulges** but face challenges in skills and stability.
- Mobility has become more complex due to visa restrictions and lifestyle preferences post-COVID.

Investors now prioritise regions that can attract, retain, and train the right people.
That means places with:

- accessible housing and lifestyle amenities;
- affordable childcare and education;
- inclusive, welcoming communities;
- partnerships between employers, educators, and councils to build skills pipelines.

For local governments, this reinforces that economic development is inseparable from liveability. Workforce attraction, housing, and amenity are now as critical to investment attraction as land and infrastructure.

5. ESG and the Rise of Responsible Investment

Environmental, Social, and Governance (ESG) considerations are no longer corporate add-ons they're central to capital decisions.

Investors, particularly institutional funds, now demand evidence of:

- low-carbon operations;
- ethical supply chains;
- workforce diversity and wellbeing;
- transparent governance and community engagement.

Regions that can demonstrate strong ESG credentials (not just talk about them) are more likely to attract high-quality, long-term investors. That means tracking and reporting community outcomes, sustainability metrics, and social licence with the same rigour as financial data. For councils and agencies, it's an opportunity to align local development goals with global investment standards and creating places that are profitable *and* principled.

6. The Investor's Changing Mindset

Investors today are not just looking for cost savings or market access. They're looking for **partnerships that de-risk decision-making**.

They want to work with regions that can:

- help navigate regulation and community expectations;
- provide stable, clean energy;
- ensure data integrity and digital resilience;
- demonstrate social licence and reputational strength.

And their risk appetites differ.

Some investors now **prefer to pilot and scale**, testing locations with smaller operations before expanding. This approach reduces exposure in uncertain global conditions. Others are still willing to go **"all in"**, committing large capital upfront, especially where they see long-term certainty in energy, workforce, and governance.

Understanding these risk profiles helps practitioners tailor engagement. Pilot investors need flexible space, responsive approvals, and fast feedback loops. All-in investors need depth (infrastructure, workforce pipelines, and political stability).

Both require professionalism and partnership.

7. The Role of Technology in Investment Decision-Making

AI and data analytics aren't just transforming industries; they're transforming *how investors choose locations*.

Most corporate site-selection teams now use AI-powered platforms that aggregate data from hundreds of sources: labour costs, connectivity, community sentiment, even satellite imagery. This means your region's **digital footprint** is as important as your physical one. If your economic data isn't accurate, consistent, and machine-readable, AI models may not "see" you or may misrepresent you entirely.

Practitioners must think beyond SEO to **Generative Engine Optimisation (GEO)**, ensuring that when AI systems generate summaries about your region, the information is correct, positive, and up to date.

This is an emerging frontier of investment promotion and those who adapt early will gain disproportionate visibility.

8. Localising the Global Shifts

While these global forces can feel abstract, they translate directly to local practice.
For councils and regional agencies, the implications are clear:

- **Integrate sustainability into everything.** Renewable energy, circular economy practices, and resilience planning are now essential components of competitiveness.
- **Build data capability.** Maintain accurate, accessible data dashboards to support both human and AI-driven site selection.
- **Focus on people.** Invest in liveability, skills, and inclusion, because capital follows talent.
- **Collaborate for scale.** Partner with neighbours, states, and industry to offer investors cohesive ecosystems.
- **Plan for agility.** Global shocks will continue. Build systems that can pivot quickly without losing direction.

In a volatile world, preparedness and adaptability are the new measures of confidence.

9. The New Geography of Investment

The convergence of these trends is reshaping geography itself.

- **Energy geography** is redefining where industries locate near cheaper and sustainable energy sources.
- **Data geography** is emerging and where server farms and digital backbones dictate investment patterns.
- **Human geography** — driven by talent, lifestyle, and remote work is dispersing opportunity beyond major cities.

For regional Australia, this presents extraordinary potential. With abundant renewable resources, lifestyle appeal, and relative political stability, regions can compete for high-value investment like never before provided they're ready, connected, and confident.

A Final Reflection

The nature of investment is evolving from extraction to innovation, from competition to collaboration, from short-term gain to long-term resilience.

For practitioners, the challenge and opportunity is to evolve with it. To think globally but act locally. To build places that attract capital not because they're the cheapest, but because they're the most capable, sustainable, and trusted.

The next decade will belong to regions that combine **digital intelligence**, **cheaper energy**, and **human connection**. Regions that understand that prosperity is no longer just about growth, but about *resilience, adaptability, and shared value*.

Because in this changing world, investors aren't simply looking for a place to build.
They're looking for a place to **belong** and a region whose vision, capability, and integrity mirror their own.

Glossary

Key Terms in Investment Attraction and Economic Development

Aftercare
The ongoing support provided to investors after they have established operations, helping them overcome challenges, connect locally, and reinvest or expand in the region.

All-In Investor
An investor who commits substantial capital and operations from the outset, rather than starting with a small pilot or trial phase.

Anchor Tenant / Anchor Employer
A large or strategically important business that attracts suppliers, workers, or customers to a location and stimulates further investment.

Benchmarking
Comparing a region's performance, infrastructure, or competitiveness against similar regions or global peers to identify strengths and gaps.

Brownfield Site
Previously developed land (such as an industrial or commercial site) that may be underutilised, vacant, or contaminated, but has redevelopment potential.

Business Retention and Expansion (BRE)
A structured program that supports existing businesses to stay, grow, and reinvest locally and are often the foundation of aftercare.

Circular Economy
An approach to economic development that minimises waste and maximises reuse, recycling, and regeneration of resources.

Cluster
A concentration of related businesses, suppliers, and institutions in a particular industry or field that benefits from shared knowledge and infrastructure.

Community Readiness
The extent to which a local community understands and supports potential investment or growth and a critical element of social licence.

Concierge Model
A facilitation approach that gives investors a single point of contact who coordinates across departments and makes doing business easier.

Critical Minerals
Minerals essential to modern technologies (e.g., lithium, rare earths, cobalt) that are central to renewable energy and manufacturing supply chains.

Customer Relationship Management (CRM) System
A database used to record and track investor enquiries, leads, contacts, and project stages throughout the investment pipeline.

Data Literacy
The ability to understand, interpret, and use data to inform decisions, communicate trends, and build evidence for policy or investment cases.

Decarbonisation
The process of reducing carbon emissions through clean energy, improved efficiency, and sustainable practices.

Due Diligence
The process of verifying financial, legal, and operational information before finalising an investment or partnership.

Ecosystem (Investment Ecosystem)
The network of partners, policies, institutions, and assets that collectively enable investment attraction, facilitation, and retention in a region.

Environmental, Social, and Governance (ESG)
A framework used by investors to assess an organisation or region's sustainability, ethics, and governance standards.

Facilitation
The process of helping investors navigate regulatory, planning, and operational systems so that investment decisions and implementations occur smoothly.

Focus Sectors
Priority industries or clusters a region targets for investment, based on comparative advantage, strategic fit, or community goals.

Generative Engine Optimisation (GEO)
The emerging practice of ensuring that AI systems (like ChatGPT or Gemini) access accurate, positive, and up-to-date information about a region. Similar in concept to Search Engine Optimisation (SEO), but for AI-generated content.

Greenfield Site
Undeveloped land identified for new investment, typically free of prior structures and constraints.

Incentives
Financial or non-financial advantages offered to investors to reduce risk or cost, such as rate relief, fast-tracked approvals, or training support.

Industry Development
The broader process of supporting growth within specific industries or clusters through capability-building, infrastructure, and policy alignment.

Infrastructure Readiness
The extent to which a region's physical and digital infrastructure (energy, water, transport, broadband) can support new investment.

Innovation Ecosystem
The network of research institutions, businesses, and investors that supports entrepreneurship, technology transfer, and product development.

Investment Attraction
The proactive process of promoting a region, identifying investors, and facilitating projects that bring capital, jobs, and skills to a community.

Investment Facilitation Charter
A formal statement or framework that outlines how a region engages with investors (roles, timelines, responsibilities, and service standards).

Investment Pipeline
The portfolio of potential, active, and committed investment projects being managed by an economic development organisation.

Investment Readiness
A measure of how well-prepared a region is to attract and

deliver investment, including sites, infrastructure, governance, community support, and internal processes.

Knowledge Sharing
The intentional exchange of information, lessons, and best practices among practitioners, partners, and stakeholders.

Lead Generation
The process of identifying, engaging, and nurturing potential investors who align with a region's strategic priorities.

Local Content
Goods, services, or labour sourced from within a region, often used to measure local benefit or participation in major projects.

Pilot Investment
A smaller-scale or trial investment that allows a company to test a region's suitability before committing to larger expansion.

Qualifying Investor
An investor assessed as credible, aligned, and feasible under an organisation's qualification or prioritisation framework.

Qualification Matrix
A structured tool used to evaluate and score investor enquiries based on criteria such as alignment, feasibility, impact, and risk.

Readiness Review
A regular internal process that checks whether a region's data, infrastructure, and systems remain up to date and capable of supporting new investment.

Resilience
The capacity of a region, economy, or system to absorb

shocks, adapt to change, and recover stronger after disruption.

Site Visit
An in-person inspection where investors visit potential locations, meet stakeholders, and assess suitability and is often a decisive step in site selection.

Social Licence
The level of community acceptance and trust that allows an investment or project to operate successfully and sustainably.

Stakeholder Engagement
The process of consulting, informing, and collaborating with people or groups affected by or involved in economic development activities.

Supply Chain Mapping
Identifying local businesses that can supply or benefit from investment projects. Often used to demonstrate regional capacity and economic linkages.

Sustainability
The integration of environmental, social, and economic considerations to ensure long-term viability and responsible growth.

Unique Value Proposition (UVP)
A clear, evidence-based statement of what makes a region distinctive, credible, and attractive to investors — its core "why here?" message.

Value-Add
The additional economic contribution created by transforming inputs into higher-value outputs, often measured as Gross Regional Product (GRP) impact.

Workforce Readiness
The preparedness of a region's labour force to meet current and future industry needs, including skills, training pathways, and housing availability.

Acknowledgements

Writing this book has been as much about reflection as it has been about research. It represents the collective experience of countless conversations, projects, and partnerships across Australia and beyond and it simply wouldn't exist without the generosity, trust, and collaboration of many people along the way.

To the **economic development practitioners** in local councils, regional organisations, industry groups, and state agencies who shared their challenges, lessons, and wins with me: thank you. You are the true architects of community prosperity. The honesty and commitment you bring to your work continue to inspire me daily.

To the **mentors and peers** who have challenged and encouraged me throughout my career people like *Derek Ephrem, Scott Templeman, Paul Martins, Alex Lever-Shaw, David Camerlengo, and the many colleagues and leaders* in the field of Economic Development, Investment Attraction and Site Selection your example and insight have shaped my thinking more than you realise.

To the **communities I've worked with** from remote towns to growing cities thank you for reminding me that investment attraction is never about numbers alone. It's about people, purpose, and pride in place.

To my **friends and family**, who have patiently read my endless drafts *Carolyn Cranch, Nichola Warburton, Andrea Kanaris* thank you for your support and encouragement. You've been the quiet constant behind everything I do.

And finally, to the next generation of economic development professionals and community leaders (the people reading this book) thank you for caring about this work. Thank you for choosing a profession that demands both heart and rigour, vision and patience.

If this book helps you see your community's potential a little more clearly or gives you the tools and confidence to bring one more investment to life, then it's achieved its purpose.

Because, in the end, the real story of economic development isn't written in reports or strategies. It's written in the jobs created, the businesses grown, and the belief built. One region, one project, and one practitioner at a time.

About the Author

Paul Cranch is an experienced economic development professional, consultant, and thought leader dedicated to helping communities turn local potential into lasting prosperity.

Based in Queensland, Paul has spent his career working with councils, regional organisations, and state agencies to strengthen local economies, attract investment, and build capability within the profession. His work combines a deep understanding of on-the-ground realities with a strategic grasp of the forces reshaping global investment, from renewable energy and digitalisation to demographic and geopolitical change.

Paul is the founder of **Local Economic Impact Advisory**, an independent consultancy focused on **data-driven strategy and place-based impact**. Through his work, he partners with governments to develop practical tools and programs that make investment attraction, facilitation, and aftercare achievable in real-world contexts.

He is also a recognised voice in the field through his suite of professional newsletters (*EcDev with Paul*, *EcDev Jobs*, and *EcDev Data)* which reach thousands of subscribers across Australia and internationally. These platforms reflect his mission to connect, inform, and elevate the economic development profession through accessible, evidence-based insights.

Before returning to Australia, Paul spent more than a decade in Japan, where he studied commerce in Japanese at Kansai University and built a career in brand management and international business development. That experience shaped his global perspective and continues to inform his approach to cross-cultural partnerships, investment facilitation, and place branding.

An advocate for professional development and collaboration, Paul contributes regularly to **Economic Development Australia (EDA)** and international networks such as the **International Economic Development Council (IEDC)**. His work emphasises capability-building, community readiness, and practical leadership. Equipping practitioners to meet the evolving challenges of economic development with confidence, competence, and integrity.

When he's not writing, mentoring, or advising, Paul can often be found training at CrossFit, volunteering in Brisbane's Japanese community, or travelling across regional Australia exploring the stories that shape local economies.

Local Economic Impact Advisory
Data-driven strategy. Place-based impact.
www.ecdev.com.au